Know-How
for Family
Lawyers

Know-How for Family Lawyers

First Edition

Diana Parker
Partner, Withers , London

Richard Sax
Partner, Rubinstein Callingham Polden & Gale, London

Peggy Ray
Partner, Goodman Ray, London

Editor
Jenny Franklin
Solicitor

© Longman Group UK Ltd 1993

ISBN 0 75200 0063

Published by
Longman Law, Tax and Finance
Longman Group UK Ltd
21–27 Lamb's Conduit Street
London WC1N 3NJ

Associated offices
Australia, Hong Kong, Malaysia, Singapore, USA

A CIP catalogue record for this book is available from the British Library.

Printed in Great Britain by Bell and Bain Ltd., Glasgow

Contents

Preface

This book is not going to tell you the law— there are plenty of large and worthy text books around to do that. What it will do is pass on know-how and expertise that is only acquired through years of practice. It gives guidance on how to handle the case itself, the clients, solicitors on the other side of a case and the office of a family lawyer.

The first chapter concentrates on the solicitor and his team, focusing on the right approach to family law, knowledge and skills, organising the work and the solicitor's relationship with the client. The next question to be looked at is client care—fundamental to a good and successful practice. This includes a detailed consideration of the all-important first interview which will set the tone for the rest of the case.

Each case will have its own detail which distinguishes it from all others (this is one of the particular interests of family law practice) so that in many instances the advice given is broad-brush rather than specific. The intention is, however, to give the reader a series of guidelines to follow and to raise markers where there may be unforeseen dangers or difficulties for the less experienced practitioner.

In Chapter 3 we consider strategy, including such matters as timing, bringing in of experts and dealing with difficult solicitors. Chapter 4 deals with negotiation. With the growing emphasis on a conciliatory approach to family disputes and the incentive to save costs for the client where possible, negotiation skills are a vital part of the solicitor's expertise. The subject of Chapter 5 is litigation where we have concentrated mainly on the practicalities of preparing for a contested hearing.

We then consider mediation—an attractive and increasingly available alternative for many clients who wish to resolve their difficulties amicably. We examine the schemes currently available and consider the solicitor's role during and after mediation, as well as looking at mediation as a new discipline and area of work for the solicitor.

In the following three chapters grouped together under the general heading of 'Specific Areas' we have concentrated on the most significant areas of work commonly undertaken under the general umbrella of family law: child related cases, financial provision, divorce and emergency proceedings. We have tried to look at important issues which will affect most practitioners in the field and to focus on aspects which prove problematic. Some major areas, such as cohabitation and inheritance provision have had to be omitted while others, the new Child Support Act 1991 and welfare law for example, have been only touched upon. Space has not permitted otherwise.

Chapter 10 is devoted to legal aid and is intended to provide a practical guide for the practitioner unfamiliar with the workings of the system.

Last, but by no means least, we have looked in Chapter 11 at the all-important management and organisational aspects of the business. While much of what is said applies generally to private practice, we have concentrated on those matters which apply particularly to family law practitioners who are either considering setting up their own firm or who are part of an existing department in a larger firm. We wish to emphasise that we have not set out to provide a comprehensive guide to running a business but to pass on personal experience in this field.

We would like to thank Frances Hughes and also Joanna Bosanquet, Jackie Wells, Marcus Dearle and Jane Gorvin for their helpful suggestions in the early stages of this book, and particularly Haema Sundram and Lyn Ayrton who very kindly read the manuscript.

By way of convention we have tended to refer to the client and to the solicitor as 'he'—please read this as implying male or female. Similarly the term 'solicitor' will embrace any practitioner, eg legal executive, trainee or clerk.

Diana Parker
Richard Sax
Peggy Ray
Jenny Franklin

September 1993

1 The Solicitor and his Team

1 The Solicitor and his Team

1.1 Approach

1.1.1 Particular features of family law

This is an area of practice where there is less emphasis on law and more on an understanding of wider issues, giving an opportunity to deal directly with personal matters deeply affecting the client. It is stressful work because it involves dealing with deeply felt emotions and is not for the faint-hearted or impatient. It is important to realise that, contrary to many clients' expectations, you cannot wave a magic wand and resolve their difficulties. It is not an area of law in which you will be richly rewarded financially—for where you can expect always to receive gratitude from the client however good a job you know you have done for the client.

1.1.2 The right approach

It is widely accepted that the good family law practitioner's role is to encourage his client to adopt a conciliatory approach to the resolution of the dispute facing him and his family. This will involve explaining to him the detrimental effect that a litigious manner of conducting the case will have on all the family and in particular on any children of the family. The solicitor must also ensure that throughout the case the interests of any children involved are treated as a priority. This approach is underlined by the relevant legislation (Children Act 1989) which encourages adults to remain parents through the process of family breakdown rather than protagonists in a battle. Research has shown that children fare much better in the longer term in cases where parents have been able to deal in a civilised manner with each other; clients often need to be reminded of this.

Guidance as to the practical application of such an approach is to be found in the Code of Practice of The Solicitor's Family Law Association (SFLA) (*see* section 1 of Appendix 7). The Association was founded in 1982 by a group of solicitors in response to growing concern about the direction family law was taking and a conviction that family law needed, where possible, to move away from adversarial positions towards an emphasis on a conciliatory approach, to the ultimate benefit of the whole family. Since its inception the SFLA has grown rapidly and now has some 3,000 members throughout the country. Its aims and objectives are stated *inter alia* to be:

> 'to encourage solicitors to represent their clients in a manner which promotes the sensitive and economic handling of the family disputes and assist individuals to reconcile their differences, and to seek solutions fair to all members of the family and to the children in particular.'

The authors of this book are all members of the SFLA, and the approach endorsed by the SFLA underlies all that is said. Anyone unfamiliar with the Code should study it carefully.

It should be pointed out that favouring a conciliatory approach to family law work does not imply a fear of litigation and a willingness to settle at all costs. Robust litigation has its place and the solicitor must judge when that is an appropriate course to take (*see* Chapters 4 and 5).

1.1.3 What makes a good family law solicitor?

Given the particular demands of the job, you will find yourself needing to demonstrate certain qualities over and above those associated with the legal profession in general. You will need, in addition to a thorough knowledge of family law and particular specialisms within that area, a familiarity with a large number of other areas of the law, eg welfare benefits, conveyancing, the law of trusts, tax law, pensions, company law, and the wider context in which you are dealing. In order to run a case well and profitably you will need to be an efficient organiser both of your own time and of those working for you. In your relationship with the client you will need a great deal of patience, a sense of humour, to be able to put up with being shouted at by a client who has no one else to shout at, and the ability to remain detached while not appearing indifferent.

Finally, you will need to be secure within yourself, to know your own limits and when to refer the client for further help to other experts, and to be able to keep work and its attendant stresses and strains apart from the rest of your life.

1.2 Knowledge and skills

1.2.1 Knowing the law and procedure

In addition to having a good working knowledge of family law and procedure, you must also know where to find the information you do not carry in your head. A list of useful reference works is included in Appendix 1. It is helpful also for all members of a department to be equipped with separate copies of the most important Acts, eg Matrimonial Causes Act 1973 (MCA 1973), Matrimonial and Family Proceedings Act 1984 (FPA 1984), Children Act 1989 (CA 1989), and Rules (particularly Family Proceedings Rules 1991 (FPR 1991)), for ease of reference. Make sure that you are up to date with all amendments. The Family Law Reports, while not essential regular reading, are nevertheless a valuable resource, particularly in a firm where the solicitor is likely to be doing a fair amount of advocacy. The Law Society's *Guide to the Professional Conduct of Solicitors* (6th edn) and *Professional Standards Bulletin* are very useful regarding matters of professional conduct.

It can be helpful to keep old books carefully segregated in case you are asked to deal with a matter which relates to repealed legislation. However, be very careful that old editions are clearly marked as such and be sure to check that the edition you use is the appropriate one for each case. You should also ensure that you are familiar with local court practices and procedures which can vary from court to court, eg use of pre-trial reviews in ancillary relief applications.

1.2.2 Journals and periodicals

Keeping up to date is crucial and is hard work. The journal Family Law is required reading. The SFLA produces a quarterly newsletter for its members. Useful articles and information are found also in the *Law Society's Gazette* and the *Solicitor's Journal*. The *Child Care Practitioner's Guide* published by Remy Zemtar is very useful. Read *The Times* Law Reports regularly and photocopy for future reference. Circulate anything you see of interest anywhere to other members of the department.

1.2.3 Seminars

Seminars are a useful way of keeping in touch with recent changes in the law and developing specific or general practice skills—indeed

the Law Society training requirements include compulsory attendance at a certain number of training courses annually for solicitors
qualifying after 1 August 1987.

Select one member of the department to be responsible for considering what is available, with a careful eye towards content and quality of lecturers. Assess whether the seminar will concentrate on
theory or on practical matters and select according to your requirements. There are now many seminars to choose from and not all are
highly regarded. Pay careful attention to the cost. SFLA seminars
tend to be particularly good value. Those organised by the SFLA
Education Committee concentrate on the wider issues of family law,
such as negotiating skills or dealing with the difficult client, while
the Training Committee seminars deal with information, eg Child
Support Act 1991.

It is common practice to send one member of a firm to a seminar
and to arrange for him to pass on his newly acquired knowledge to
the other members of the department. You may consider the possibility of arranging seminars for a group of local firms.

Multi-disciplinary seminars and courses run by organisations
such as London Marriage Guidance Council (Relate), the Institute of
Marital Studies, the Council for Family Proceedings, the NSPCC
and NAGALRO (National Association of Guardians *ad litem* and
Reporting Officers), while not necessarily aimed specifically at solicitors, can be extremely helpful in broadening the solicitor's understanding of the area in which he is working. It is essential,
particularly in work relating to children, to be multidisciplinary in
your approach to your work (Cleveland Report).

1.2.4   In-house lectures and meetings

While few firms will have a family law department large enough to
justify specialist in-house lectures, lectures on general skills, eg
client interviewing and negotiating skills, can be effective even in a
small firm. Consider also the possibility of lunch time lectures for the
secretarial staff on legal issues so that they have a clearer understanding of those matters with which they deal on a daily basis.
Greater insight will lead to greater involvement in secretarial work
and a better service to you and the client.

Weekly departmental meetings where information can be shared
and difficulties aired may be practical/useful in your firm. Even if

regular meeting are not held, it is a good idea to circulate notes or copies of counsel's opinion on matters of general application.

1.2.5 Networking

It is well worth giving the time and energy to making and maintaining contact with a wide circle of other professionals working both in your particular field and in related areas. As well as other solicitors these may include counsel, mediators, conciliators, psychiatrists and social workers. Join the SFLA which also provides social and educational benefits. Keep your own directory of useful contacts and keep in touch with them, eg Christmas cards. Remember that networking is a two-way process and that you must be prepared to give time to requests made to you. There are significant benefits, particularly to the solicitor practising on his own or in a small department. You never know when you might need to find a Kurdish child psychiatrist or just simply to let off steam!

1.2.6 Specialisms

The development of specialist areas of practice within the field of family law will set your firm apart from others and will enable you to attract clients and offer them a better service. Any firm is large enough to sustain some specialisms. Your choice of specialisms will be dictated largely by the type of firm you are in, its location and the type of clients it attracts or wishes to attract.

Look at growing areas, eg cohabitation, international cases and pensions. Other areas you might consider include matrimonial finance and taxation, trust law, children (public or private law, adoption, child abduction), Inheritance Act claims, immigration, enforcement, domestic violence, or welfare benefits.

1.2.7 Recognising the limits of your expertise

You need to be able to recognise matters which you are unable to deal with yourself. Do not be embarrassed to seek assistance either from someone else within your firm, from counsel or from a solicitor in another firm, or if the client's difficulties are not primarily legal difficulties, to refer him to the appropriate agency (*see* Chapter 2).

1.3   Organising the work

1.3.1   General

Every practitioner needs to be able to organise his work efficiently but this is crucial in the face of the demands of family law and what is likely to be, especially in legal aid practices, a very heavy case load. It is therefore important that you build up individual and departmental administrative systems which are reliable. Only with a high degree of organisation can you hope to deal satisfactorily with the emergencies which invariably arise in family law work.

1.3.2   Balancing administration and case work

It is important also to keep clearly in mind the balance between your duties to the client and to the business. You can only give the best service to your clients if you, your department and your firm are well organised and running efficiently and profitably. Administrative tasks may have to wait until the end of the day but they must be dealt with and recognised as being ultimately of benefit not only to the firm but also to the client. It is a matter of making priorities and keeping to them under pressure.

1.3.3   Pressure from the client

There is particular pressure from clients in family law work for the solicitor to deal with their own problem immediately. You must be able to remain calm in such circumstances, to keep a clear idea of the relative urgency in dealing with each case and with different aspects of each case, and to explain the position firmly to the client. It will often be enough simply to explain to the client that immediate pressure of work does not allow you to deal with his less urgent matter immediately. Try to give a clear and realistic indication of when you will be able to give his case attention and stick to it.

Efficiency also means dealing firmly with the client who wishes to tell you every last detail of his life history, which may be fascinating but irrelevant to the case (*see* Chapter 2).

1.3.4 Some practical aspects of organisation

Diary

Keeping a diary is essential. Not only should it contain dates of all court hearings and meetings, but it should also be marked up with reminders to allow adequate time for preparation. Highlighting in different colours is helpful. In addition to the solicitor's personal diary there should be a court diary for the use of the whole department. If then it transpires for example that the firm has two appointments at the same court on the same day it may be possible for one person to deal with them both. It may be helpful to hold weekly or fortnightly diary meetings to deal with such matters. A five–year diary may be helpful.

It need hardly be said that the diary will be of little use without a proper system for ensuring that dates are entered in the appropriate diaries. Deal rigorously with those aspects of the diary that are within your control, eg setting aside time for administration or drafting an affidavit, and making sure appointments are not piled up too closely. Take the time to dictate yourself reminders of matters other than diary dates that must be dealt with, eg compliance with court directions and reminders of when statements and documents etc are expected from the other party.

Checking case list

Check your case list regularly to make sure that nothing has been overlooked. Your firm's computer system may be programmed to provide printouts of useful information, including unbilled work in progress or the absence of any transactions on the file for a particular period of time. It is also useful to organise regular checks, say every month, through your filing cabinet to ensure that inactive files are not overlooked. Do not rely on your memory—it does not always work!

Use of precedents

Use precedents wherever possible, and build up a personal or departmental system. This can include most court forms, standard letters, your client care letters and mandatory legal aid letters. It also assists in maintaining a high standard of documentation throughout the firm and ensures a consistent approach.

File management

This includes keeping each file tidy and up to date. Not only will this save you time but it enables a colleague to deal with the matter if necessary. This is particularly important if more than one person is dealing with the case. Leave legible notes and a case summary in the file so that the next person to pick up the file can quickly ascertain the current position. Ensure that the file is well organised and tidy, eg by keeping pleadings, your documents, other side's documents etc, in separate envelopes, plastic folders or pins. It saves time to have a file sheet on the file cover giving such details as your client's telephone number and that of the other solicitor, file references, other telephone and fax numbers, legal aid certificate number, details of experts instructed and any particular features of the case clearly marked, such as when a party's address is not to be disclosed to the other party or undertakings given. Make sure that it is kept up to date.

Take the time to think each case through and make sure that all that should be happening is happening. With a legal aid matter you must also constantly watch the level of legal aid cover and plan for further extensions or applications which may have to be made.

Proper delegation (see below, para 1.3.5)

1.3.5 Working as a team

You should look upon yourself as part of a team in dealing with each case. The team may be comprised only of yourself and your secretary but you both have complementary roles to play. Often, the team will also include another member or other members of the department. It may from time to time include members of other departments of your firm with specialist skills. It is useful and cost effective to be able to select those within the department with different levels of experience and on different charging rates to work on specific matters in a particular case. For example, time consuming activities such as preparation of statements, affidavits, or court bundles should be dealt with by a member of the department with a lower charging rate than that of the principal.

There will inevitably be a small amount of overlap but with careful organisation and working practices it is possible to keep duplication to a minimum. Good file management is essential (*see above,* para **1.3.4**). Remember, however, that you must always supervise the work that you have delegated to others.

Do not forget to explain to the client how the team will work and the costs advantage to him.

Do not underestimate the secretary's role in the team. She will need the temperament and many of the qualities of the family lawyer. She will need to be able to prioritise, to know when she needs help and she must know not to advise. She will need to know how to handle the manipulative client (and solicitor!) and she must be discreet. She can also provide assistance when the client needs a friendly ear rather than legal advice.

Make sure that your team know that they are valued. Offer praise and encouragement, and share any gifts received at the end of a case from grateful clients.

1.4   Looking after oneself and one's team

1.4.1   Dealing with stress

Every solicitor practising in this field will experience stress. It should not be underestimated. There may be a great deal of emotional pressure from a particular client or you may have to listen to harrowing stories; there will be times when your client is very rude to, and critical of, you. There will be times when you feel you have more work than you can properly handle or when you simply do not know how to make progress in a particular case. You may find yourself working far into the night and achieving very little. These are all common problems even if they feel unique to you at the time. Be alert also for the symptoms of stress in your colleagues. Whatever the underlying problem, it will usually be fairly easy to pinpoint and it must be faced and resolved. Remember that it is never as difficult as you thought it was going to be beforehand.

The first and most important step to take, whatever the problem and however senior you may be, is to discuss it with someone else, be it your principal or another member of the department. In some instances discussing a difficulty with a colleague or even merely describing it can present a hitherto unrecognised solution. It may be appropriate to pass over a particular file which is troubling you to another member of the department, so long as this is presented carefully to the client. If you have a particularly heavy case load and you can see that it is a temporary difficulty only, it may be possible to redistribute the work in the department; or it may be necessary to think of taking on another assistant if it is a longer term problem.

If there is no one to whom you feel able to unburden yourself, the Professional Standards Directorate of the Law Society can put you in touch with a member of the solicitors' assistance scheme who is available to talk confidentially about any problems a solicitor may be experiencing. The scheme is operated by Law Society members but is separate from the Law Society.

(*See also* Chapter 2—dealing with the difficult client, para **2.5**)

1.4.2 Looking after yourself

This is important. Take regular holidays and make sure that you have free time away from the demands of the work during the week. If you have to work at weekends try to ensure that you set aside one day or part of both days for other things. Try to be aware of the distinction between working long hours because a particular case or circumstances demand it and working merely because you are in the habit of doing so.

There are many potentially stressful situations that you can take basic measures to avoid by ensuring, for instance, that as far as possible your client appointments are spread at intervals through the day. Do not be tempted to take on more cases than you can handle— a new client may well be prepared to wait to see you if you are able personally to explain the position to him and are able to fix an appointment in, say, two or three weeks. It is often difficult to say no to a potential client who may have a harrowing tale and needs help, but it will be of no service to him if you take on the case and then cannot deal with it properly.

1.4.3 Mistakes

It is impossible to avoid all mistakes and everyone makes them from time to time. Most are easily remedied. There are, however, ways of reducing the likelihood of mistakes occurring and it is important not to allow the fear of making errors to make you practice defensively, eg going to counsel unnecessarily. These include the following;

(a) Make sure that you have personal and departmental systems that you can rely on (eg the diary for court dates, guaranteed delivery of telephone messages, keeping notes of meetings and telephone conversations).

(b) If you are the head of department, read all incoming mail so that you know what is going on. This is a good way of picking up potential problems, eg in the form of aggressive correspondence from clients or other solicitors which can then be dealt with at an early opportunity. This should be seen as reassuring by other members of the department rather than the reverse.

(c) Do not make assumptions about a case—check regularly that you are proceeding in the right way legally and tactically and in accordance with the client's wishes.

(d) Do not follow counsel's advice blindly—mistakes are sometimes made.

(e) Do not be pressurised by the client into taking steps on his behalf which you know or feel are not right.

(f) Be sure that you alert someone else if you are in any difficulty and that every member of your team is instructed to do the same. If you realise that something has gone wrong it is essential that you are straightforward with your client. Do not take a defensive line. Offer an apology and a constructive plan to take the case forward. For formal complaints procedure and responding to a client's complaint, *see* Chapter 2.

If there is a potential negligence claim, be honest with your client. Tell him to take advice from another solicitor and that you will be as co-operative as possible.

1.5   The solicitor/client relationship

1.5.1   Reassuring the client

Family law is one area of practice where your client may never have had dealings with a solicitor before. He or she is likely to be suffering considerable emotional stress and anxiety and it is particularly important to consider the impression that you make. Whatever his social background the client may be quite unsophisticated financially or businesswise and you should try to ensure that he does not find you intimidating.

Make it plain that you understand that he may be experiencing feelings of guilt or anger and that you are not there to make any judgement on what your client may have done or experienced. Offer sympathy in the real sense of the word—it may help to reassure your client that he is not extraordinary by referring to your own experiences or to the fact that others known to you as clients are or have been in the same position.

1.5.2   Objectivity and detachment

Remember, however, that a high degree of objectivity and detachment from the client is essential if you are to serve his best interests. Although it is important for you to recognise and allow for the emotional backdrop to the issues at hand, you must not allow yourself to become emotionally involved in the issues yourself.

It is usually inadvisable to have social contact with your client while the case is in progress. Similarly, you should not accept gifts of substantial value while the case is in progress as this may jeopardise your client's perception of your objectivity. If you feel that your relationship with a client is becoming too close and that you are becoming too involved in the case on his behalf, do not hesitate to speak to another member of the department about it. The same applies if you find that your working relationship is adversely affected by an over aggressive response to or from your client.

1.5.3   Communication

The greatest source of complaints from clients is either that they have not been informed about what is going on or that they do not understand the proceedings. It is therefore prudent to send copies of important correspondence and to advise the client of important conversations and of any delays. Avoid legal jargon—it is likely to annoy or even intimidate your client. Use plain English and address him in a manner which is intelligible but not condescending. Make sure that your client has absorbed and understood what you have said or written—sometimes his emotional state, particularly at an initial interview, may prevent him from doing so.

When acting for a child it is particularly important that your communications are regular and clear. If the child is of sufficient maturity to instruct you, he is entitled to receive his own correspondence appropriately marked 'private and confidential'. The responsibility for what goes into your correspondence is very high. You must think carefully of the context in which you are imparting information. (*See also* Chapter 7, para **7.4**)

1.5.4   Confidentiality

It is extremely important in the area of family law to be discreet and to maintain confidentiality. Resist at all costs the temptation to talk about a case to others, even if you do not name the client involved. You can never be sure what information may fall into the wrong hands. This is even more important in a local firm where the parties or their families may well be known to you and to members of your staff. Make sure also that all your staff understand how seriously you would treat any breach of confidentiality. Have a confidentiality clause in the contract of employment and explain the consequences of any breach. It is important too that you should be discreet with your own partners.

1.5.5   Off the record communications

It is generally prudent to avoid receiving 'off the record' information, ie information not to be disclosed to your client, because of the conflict between having knowledge of the information and your principal duty to the client. Distinguish 'without prejudice'—discussed in Chapter 4, para **4.7.3**).

1.5.6   Dress

Do not feel obliged to dress down for your client—even clients who are casually dressed themselves expect the professional to look the part. However it is important to retain approachability.

2 Client Care

2 Client Care

2.1 Quality of client care

Quality of client care is a well-recognised ingredient in the successful running of any legal practice. Its impact will be felt from the initial moment of contact, throughout the client's dealings with the firm and beyond. It requires particular attention from family law practitioners because of the very nature of their clients' problems.

Many of those who consult a family law solicitor will be visiting a firm of solicitors for the first time and most will be under considerable emotional stress arising from the problem that brings them to you. It is therefore important to put them at their ease as far as possible, to reassure and to inspire confidence. Bear in mind that the client is a customer and free to take his business elsewhere.

Conversely, a satisfied client is an important source of potential further business for the firm with a general private practice, as he may well need the services of the firm's conveyancing department or advice on a will or on financial matters. A satisfied client will also be an important source of new clients through his recommendation of the firm.

The tone of your relationship with your client will be set by his initial dealings with staff, the appearance of the premises and the important first meeting. All subsequent dealings require a similar degree of considered care.

2.2 First impressions

It is important that the client's first impressions of the firm and of you are favourable. You must ensure that the first contact that the client has with the firm, whether this be by telephone or when he walks in off the street, is helpful and reassuring. This means having well-trained telephonists and receptionists, who are aware of the importance of this aspect of their work and who follow a structured procedure to ascertain the nature of the client's problem and to put him in touch with the appropriate person in the firm.

Some solicitors prefer to speak to the client themselves when the initial telephone call is made so that personal contact is established immediately. Make sure that in all cases a note is made of the client's telephone number and check whether the number may be used freely. It may be necessary for the solicitor to telephone only at certain times in order to avoid the client's spouse. Ensure that the client has clear directions for finding the solicitor's office—in some cases it may be helpful to send a map.

If your firm is a local firm relying in part on clients who will walk in off the street, it is essential that you have welcoming premises and reception staff so that potential clients are not intimidated—*see* Chapter 11, para **11.4.1**.

2.3 The initial interview

2.3.1 Preliminary practicalities

Decide who should be present at the meeting. If an assistant will be involved in the case you may want him present for all or part of the meeting. To have a third person present at the first meeting may well distract the client and impede the concentration needed between you and him. The client may feel the need to play to the audience. You may find it most helpful to have the first interview on your own and to introduce your assistant and indeed the other members of your team, eg your secretary, trainee solicitor, once the meeting is over.

Think about seating arrangements. In order to put your client at ease it may be helpful not to sit in a potentially daunting position behind a large desk.

Put your client at his ease. Those not accustomed to dealing with lawyers may be apprehensive and the very nature of the problem which brings them to the solicitor may well be extremely distressing to them. Small details, such as a friendly handshake when the client comes into the room or having an ashtray on the desk, should not be overlooked. You may wish to offer a cup of refreshment. Ensure that you will not be disturbed during the meeting, eg by diverting incoming telephone calls, so that the client is assured of your full attention. This should also enhance the client's sense of confidentiality and privacy.

It may be necessary to arrange for an interpreter to be present. Try where possible to arrange for an independent interpreter, and make sure he speaks the right dialect or uses the correct sign language for the client. (*See also* Chapter 5, para **5.7.5**.)

2.3.2   Objectives

(a) to establish the facts;
(b) to ascertain the issue or issues facing the client;
(c) to consider the appropriate course of action and advise the client accordingly;
(d) to deal with the question of legal aid entitlement and legal costs;
(e) to agree a course of action;
(f) to establish a good working relationship with the client;
(g) to fix the next appointment.

2.3.3   Establishing the facts

You will probably use a standard checklist of key information to be ascertained which you or your firm have developed to deal with your type of practice. Dealing initially with routine details of names and addresses and so on can be part of the process of helping your client to relax. In some practices the client may be asked to complete a form detailing financial information prior to the meeting with the solicitor but most practitioners prefer to deal with this face to face. Where there are children it is important that you ascertain from the client all the details pertinent to an application to the Child Support Agency at the first meeting. Such an application may need to be dealt with at an early stage and you will in any event need to have a clear idea of the likely outcome of the application in order to deal with ancillary relief claims. A precedent memorandum of financial information is included at Appendix 2. It may be appropriate to alter it to meet the requirements of your own clients. In any event it will be necessary in a case where legal aid is likely to be required to complete the legal aid application at the earliest opportunity.

It is very important to be aware throughout the interview of the client's body language and to be sensitive to what remains unspoken. Watch for those issues that he skirts around and appears unwilling to confront. Particularly at an initial interview it is important to let your client tell his story and to allow him the freedom to do so without feeling hurried. However, guidance is needed and it remains essential to keep in control so that you end up with all the facts as well as a sense of the emotional issues. Remember the crucial importance of active listening—listening is never waiting for an opportunity to speak.

2.3.4   Identifying the issues

Before you can plan any strategy for the case, it is essential that you understand what the client wishes to achieve. Your client may come to you with apparently straightforward instructions. You must be able, by way of careful questioning and gentle probing, to ascertain his underlying motives in proposing a particular course of action and what he wants to achieve at the end of the day. If you conclude that those ends are best served by completely different means, it will require great skill and delicate handling on your part to explain this to your client without alienating him or causing him to lose confidence in you.

A classic example is the client who comes into the office and instructs you immediately to file a divorce petition. By the end of the hour you realise that what the client really wants is for his or her spouse to come back and that he/she is focusing on the divorce petition as a means of shocking the other spouse into returning. Beware also of the client who says at the initial interview that he/she 'only wants what is fair' or is not interested in a financial settlement but just wants a divorce. Your experience will tell you that the client is probably unlikely to express such sentiments in several months' time. Another example is the male client who, out of a sense of guilt wishes to be overly generous to his wife. You will need to point out the consequences of such an action on any future re-marriage, that it may not be in the children's best interests for their mother to be living in much more luxurious circumstances than their father.

In circumstances such as these you will need to explain to the client why he/she may be misguided. It may be the result of ignorance as to the legal as well as the practical consequences of a particular course of action or it may be a failure to imagine the likely psychological reaction of the other spouse, short-sightedness or just muddled thinking. Much will depend on your client's emotional state at the time instructions are given.What the client says he wishes to achieve may well have an emotional overlay which results either in over-decisiveness and a wish to start proceedings immediately, or at the other extreme, an inability to make any decision at all. A useful tool in this process is the bereavement graph in Appendix 3. You may need to give consideration to whether your client is in the right frame of mind at any given time to accept the advice he needs to be given and such considerations may colour the manner in which that advice is expressed.

Be careful to distinguish legal issues from other matters that you may not be able to deal with and be aware that your view of the issues, as a lawyer, may not correspond with those of your lay client. Make sure that you have a clear idea of what your client thinks about his problems and what he wants in terms of a solution to them. Ask your client too what his spouse thinks about the situation and the likely response to any action, whether there has been any previous counselling and whether some form of counselling may be appropriate before the matter is taken any further.

Endeavour to put multiple issues in some order of priority. Consider with your client the options in respect of taking matters further. Beware of rushing into the filing of proceedings. Although there are cases when this is necessary, it can set a litigious tone and put the other party on the defensive which may be counter productive in the longer term.

2.3.5 Giving advice

Explain the law and procedure in a way that is comprehensible to your client. Pitch your advice at the appropriate level. If this is the initial interview, explain your approach to the case, eg conciliatory but firm. Set out the options open to the client and, as far as you are able at this stage, the probable outcome. It is probably best to confirm the advice you give in writing afterwards. Standard leaflets setting out divorce procedure, for example, may be useful as well. Always keep detailed attendance notes, outlining advice given verbally. If on reflection, you think your advice was a little brave, correct the impression you have given as soon as possible, and in writing if the initial advice was in writing. Never be afraid to tell a client that you would prefer to reflect (or even consult with colleagues) before committing yourself—but then get back to the client promptly. In family law work it can be very difficult to work out what advice to give—often because emotionally you might want to be reassuring the client that things will be better than you fear they may be.

2.3.6 Giving unwelcome advice

However tempting it may seem at the time, for example in an effort to protect a client from further distress, never give misleading advice. You may need to choose your moment with great care. You may feel that a particular client is likely to be most receptive to unwelcome advice during the course of the first meeting. On the other hand, the client may at this stage be angry and upset at what has occurred and it may be more appropriate to wait until the anger has passed. It is essential that your client should perceive that you as his solicitor will do the very best you can for him, even if the final outcome is not what he would have wished.

2.3.7 Reconciliation

At some stage during the initial interview with a client who is seeking a divorce you should discuss with your client the possibility of reconciliation. Do not assume that because your client has a new relationship or because his/her spouse has been violent, that there is no such prospect. Feelings can often be very ambivalent.

It is also useful to explore the extent to which the other spouse may be hoping for a reconciliation. Try to explain that couples will usually be at different stages in the separation process, and how it can be productive to attempt to even out the differences in the pace at which each wants to go.

Explain to your client who is unwilling to seek counselling that marriage guidance is not about 'patching up' a broken marriage but can be a helpful forum for clarifying issues and reducing the anger that has built up. It can help a reluctant spouse to accept the breakdown of the marriage. This will enable your client to spend less fruitless time with his solicitor, thereby reducing costs.

2.3.8 Referral

Discussing the possibility of reconciliation can be a route to discussion of referral agencies. Solicitors often find it very difficult to refer clients, especially new clients, to other agencies. It is important for your client not to feel that he is trapped in a revolving door, and also important for you to feel confident that the client will return if further legal help is required. Try to emphasise that contacting another agency would not be an alternative route but an additional one, and one that should make your client's life, and your job, easier and reduce costs. The family solicitor needs to be aware of the limits of his professional skills and to be able to recognise when his client needs or would benefit from the assistance of one of the many different forms of counselling now available. Such a referral will be dependent on what services are to be found in the area, on available funds and of course on the client's willingness to participate. It may be appropriate to refer the couple together or alternatively just your own client.

Referral agencies include marriage guidance counsellors (Relate), personal counselling, family therapy, and women's aid organisations. In some cases your client's general practitioner may be able to help. A list of referral agencies, including telephone helplines is included at Appendix 4.

(For referral for mediation, *see* Chapter 6.)

You may also wish to give the client the names and addresses of a few appropriate firms of solicitors to pass on to his spouse if no other firm has yet been consulted.

2.3.9 Funding

Informing the client

The question of the funding of the case should be tackled at an early stage, usually at the first meeting and if for some exceptional reason not then, in a follow up letter immediately afterwards. In the case of legal aid this must be a priority and you will need to deal with the application form there and then or give it to your client to take away to complete (*see* Chapter 10). The client must also be advised of the effect of the statutory charge. Remember also the duty to advise a client of his entitlement to legal aid which might require referral to a legal aid firm if you do not deal with legal aid work yourself.

In all cases you should explain in writing your firm's method of charging and charging rates, the matter of recovery of costs if there is litigation and the financial limitations of costs orders. This may be included in a general client care letter dealing with terms of business (*see below*, para **2.3.10**).

Money on account

You will almost certainly wish to ask for money on account at the first meeting—it is always easier to do this at an early stage. You should explain that you will require money to be kept on account while costs are continuing to be incurred, and your billing procedure. The appropriate amount to ask for on account at the initial meeting will depend on the nature of the case, the client's current financial circumstances and the sums involved. More complex issues and larger sums will justify a more substantial payment. In any event you should ensure that at least the costs of the initial interview are covered. It will be difficult to estimate what the total costs are likely to be, but you must attempt to give guidelines, while making it clear that these may alter subsequently as the case progresses. Be conscious that an estimate may be binding.

Billing

If you intend to bill at regular intervals, say so and explain that you will need bills to be met promptly. A common complaint against solicitors, particularly in family law work, is that clients are not kept informed of how costs are mounting. It is good practice to notify a client very regularly and in writing what unbilled costs amount to, even if for some reason you are not delivering interim bills. This is particularly easy to overlook in those legal aid cases where the statutory charge may apply.

With regard to the bills themselves, ensure that you know and explain whether you mean to deliver an 'on account' interim bill or an interim bill which, although delivered at an interim stage, is for a final amount in respect of the period in question. There is a vital distinction which affects your client's ability to dispute costs at the conclusion of a case.

2.3.10 Follow-through

Make sure that before your client leaves you have agreed a course of action and that it is one that your client understands and with which he is happy. We have mentioned that it may be helpful to follow a first meeting with a letter covering the the advice given, and confirming the action you propose to take, or one dealing merely with the latter. You should in any event deal with your firm's terms of business, funding, recovery of costs, statutory charge in a legal aid case, and your firm's complaints procedure (*see* para **2.8** *below*). The Law Society's publication *Client Care—A Guide for Solicitors* (1991) contains a standard form of client care letter which you can modify for your own purposes.

It is wrong to assume that you will necessarily have to do anything other than following up the matter with a letter. In some cases your advice may be all that the client needs.

However, where action is to be taken this may include your client speaking to his/her spouse to explain that you will be writing, followed promptly by a simple letter from you saying that you have been instructed and inviting the other party to see a solicitor. In other cases a letter to the other solicitor will be appropriate. It is good practice to show the letter to your own client before it is sent and it may be useful to dictate it while your client is with you at the first meeting (*see also* Chapter 3, paras **3.2.3** and **3.2.4**).

If the case is being handled by more than one person, make sure that the client understands this and is aware of the roles assigned to all those involved. The client should be clear who has responsibility for the day to day handling of the case and the extent of the partner's involvement if the case is delegated to an assistant.

2.3.11   Fixing another meeting

It may be helpful in what is clearly an ongoing matter to fix a date there and then for your next meeting so that the client has a time frame to focus upon.

2.4   Subsequent dealings with the client

2.4.1   Keeping the client informed

It is essential that you keep your client informed about the progress of his case. In many cases the problems which you have been asked to resolve will be having a direct bearing on the client's daily existence and it will be very important to him to know that action is being taken. It may simply be a case of sending a copy of a letter with a compliments slip (*see below*, para **2.4.5**) but it will reassure your client that progress, however minimal, is being made. Be sure that you use language that your client will understand so that he feels part of the process and not merely an onlooker.

2.4.2   Negotiating with the client

There will be occasions where you will find yourself having to negotiate with your own client, perhaps with a view to agreeing a course of action, or deciding whether to accept a proposal of settlement. In such circumstances you will need to distinguish for your client the real issues beneath the inevitable emotional overlay. You must help the client to focus forward rather than backward, exposing the emotional issues so that the client recognises them as such and accepts that they cannot influence a settlement. Remind him that the court is not going to 'punish ' the other party. It may be necessary gently but firmly to bring him down from the dizzy heights of aspiration and to inject a degree of reality into his perception of what is acceptable by way of settlement. A client is likely to have a strong immediate reaction to a proposal which you may need to counter by taking him carefully through the proposal step by step before a considered response is made. It is important, however, that you let your client have his say, however unreasonable it may seem.

2.4.3   Frequency of meetings with the client

This is a matter for the individual solicitor but unnecessary meetings should be avoided. However, it may be very helpful to meet with the client when a matter of strategy has to be decided, for example if proposals are to be put to the other side. Fixing a meeting may also provide a focus. If, for example, you tell your client that you will prepare a draft affidavit, consider fixing a meeting at that time to go through the draft. This gives you the reassurance of knowing that you cannot put off the drafting indefinitely, and gives the client the reassurance of feeling that time limits are fixed.

2.4.4   Telephone technique

Much of your contact with the client will be by telephone and the following should be borne in mind:
(a) Make sure that your client understands that time spent on a telephone call is chargeable time!
(b) Explain to your client that you will not always be available to speak to him personally but that messages will be passed on and answered as promptly as possible. If the case is being handled by more than one person there may be someone else in the office who can take the call.
(c) Ensure that you do have a system for passing on messages which operates efficiently and which is able to distinguish those calls

that need an immediate response. Most divorce clients think that their case is the most urgent and important matter that you are dealing with, and to the extent the resources of the practice allow, a call returned quickly, if only to let the client know that the matter cannot be dealt with immediately, will at least give reassurance. The important thing is for the client to be confident that you will be available to help him when it really matters.

(d) Everyone has *bêtes noires*. At any one time there is likely to be at least one client who makes frequent demands and whom you would rather avoid. Whilst weaning a client from over-dependence is sensible, try to stop and analyse your own feelings in each case. Often, clients who engender negative feelings have tricky problems. Often your reaction is to your own frustration with being confronted with the fact that you do not feel entirely at ease with how you are handling the case professionally. 'Blaming the client' does not help, nor does 'running away'—the calls will only get more frantic and you will end up feeling less in control of the situation.

2.4.5   Copying correspondence to the client

Sending the client copies of inter-solicitor correspondence has the advantage of keeping the client informed of the progress of the case, but you need to be discriminating. Some clients will expect all correspondence to be copied, no matter how routine. Others will be upset by the tone of the other solicitor's letters (sometimes, almost whatever he or she writes) and it may be better to summarise instead. Try to gauge the position for each client and ask at regular intervals if the tack that you are taking feels right. It is a good idea to copy chasing letters to your client so that he knows that you are dealing with the other party's tardiness without having to be prompted.

2.4.6   Referring to the other parties in correspondence

It can sometimes be a problem to know how you should refer to your client, his or her spouse and the other solicitor. There are no hard and fast rules but many solicitors find it preferable not to adopt too informal a tone in addressing their own clients. Likewise, it is good practice to refer to your client's spouse simply as 'your husband' or 'your former husband', etc. You should bear in mind the client's likely perception of the relationship between you and the other side's solicitor if an informal 'Dear John' style is adopted. Try to avoid referring critically to your client's spouse or his solicitor even when your client is doing so.

2.5 The difficult client

Difficult clients come in all shapes and sizes. It may be a matter of chemistry as much as anything, or the history of your relationship, leading to mutual defensiveness and criticism. If you have a specialist colleague, talk through the problems, and consider using him or her to see whether a new face makes for a less difficult client.

Often you will have to plough on. Remember that the clients you like are those that you will want to do well for, and the clients that you do not like are the ones you will simply have to do well for.

As hinted at in the section on telephone technique above, difficult clients can assume dimensions out of all proportion, often because an irritating behavioural trait is coupled with a case which is technically difficult or one where you feel that you must have made mistakes, and therefore prefer to avoid. Try to grasp where the difficulty lies.

You may feel that you are being manipulated, or overburdened by indecisiveness. If so, set the ground rules. If you are finding your client impossible, he or she may be finding you impossible. Sometimes it can be helpful to allow for the fact that there is a problem to be referred to; that way, you can try to establish a *modus vivendi* for the future. This is a technique which needs to be handled with caution, however.

Problems may also arise with the capricious client who is constantly changing the instructions he gives you. Explain to him that the court will find it much more difficult to give a client what he wants if the client is uncertain and has changed his mind several times during the course of the proceedings. Explain to your client the impact of such behaviour on the case as a whole, not least upon the question of costs. Point out the implications of a change in plan, without pressurising. Make sure with such clients that at the end of a meeting you reiterate what you intend to do, invite the client to think about it overnight and make it clear that, unless you hear from him to the contrary the following day, you will act as agreed.

2.6   The child as client

See Chapter 7, para **7.4**.

2.7   Cultural differences

There are countless examples of cultural and religious differences of which the solicitor needs to be aware in order to provide a sensitive and caring service for a client. The following are but a few examples: the female client who never comes to see you herself but is always represented by her father or brother, the significance to the client of family jewellery, the different views of women's rights and place in society, or acceptable child care practices in different societies. Other differences are less immediately apparent, but should not be under-estimated.

Religious beliefs and cultural practices will colour a client's whole approach to his present family problems and may influence both the instructions given to you and the attitude taken to any decision made by the court. It is not infrequent that a client may suddenly withdraw instructions and reach an agreement directly with the other party or through the mediation of family or community, only to come back to you subsequently when the agreement fails. In many instances it may be very difficult to resist the temptation to be judgmental.

You may need to give particular consideration to the manner in which the dispute is resolved in order to accommodate religious beliefs. This is most likely to arise in connection with the dissolution of the marriage itself, such as the particular rules relating to a Jewish Get (Jewish divorce).

In some cases your strategy for the case will need to reflect the cultural expectations of your client, perhaps for example in relation to a financial resolution following divorce. There may be existing complex family arrangements regarding the holding of property or the repayment of debts; inter-family financial transactions may not be recorded and therefore difficult to prove. In such cases it will be necessary to look at financial provision from the point of view of standard of living.

It is particularly important in all such cases to ensure that you give clear, written advice to your client and that he has the means of understanding it, if necessary through an interpreter (for information on obtaining an interpreter *see* Chapter 5, para **5.7.5**). It is helpful to have a general understanding of how the community to which your client belongs is organised, the role of the extended family, customary family arrangements and if you need to take such advice on a specific issue affecting the case it should be covered by legal aid where your client has a certificate. A useful source of such information may be a local social worker within the community concerned. For advice on religious issues your client may be advised to contact the appropriate organisation, such as the Jewish Marriage Council or the Catholic Marriage Advisory Council, or the Council of Sharia (for Muslims).

A helpful reference work is *English Law and Ethnic Minority Customs* by S M Poulter (Butterworths 1986).

2.8 Dealing with clients' complaints

2.8.1 Formal complaints procedure

Your firm will have a complaints handling procedure which the client will have been informed of by letter at the outset of the case (*see above*, para **2.3.10**). The Law Society recommendations for such a procedure are to be found in Appendix F to The Law Society's *Client Care Guide*. These include naming a person to whom the client should address his complaint in the first instance—probably the partner responsible for the case. If the complaint concerns him then it may be the department head, and a further member of the firm, such as the managing partner or senior partner if the client is still not satisfied. There should be a specified time limit for responding to any complaint, which may include an invitation to a meeting to discuss the matter. If the client still remains unsatisfied, he should be informed of his right to apply to the Solicitors Complaints Bureau.

2.8.2 Responding to complaints

When a client initially raises a complaint you should listen carefully to what he has to say and respond positively. Tell him that you are sorry to hear that he takes that view and that you will talk to the partner concerned about the matter. Often merely telling the client that you are willing to discuss the matter with your superior will reassure him and prevent the matter going any further. In any event make sure that you are not immediately defensive as this will only make matters more difficult for the client.

2.8.3   Complaints about bills

Make sure that you are familiar with the procedures set out in the Solicitors Acts for dealing with complaints about costs and that the statutory notice is stamped or printed on your bills.

3 Strategy

3 Strategy

3.1 The client's wishes and emotional state

Before any strategy can be worked out, it is essential that the solicitor understands what the client really wishes to achieve. This is frequently not as straightforward as it sounds. There may be an overlay of anger, guilt or deep grief leading to confusion of long term wishes with short term measures—refer to Chapter 2.

Be conscious of what stage in the process of coming to terms with the matter in issue the other client has reached as well as your own. You may well have to remind your client that while he has been planning, say, separation or divorce over a period of time, the suggestion may come as a complete shock to the other party, who will then need time to adjust to the idea, to 'catch up' as it were, and that it is in your client's best interests to allow this process to occur and not to force the pace.

3.2 First lines of strategy

3.2.1 Do nothing

It is very important not to feel that strategy must involve action. It is often the case, except where there is a real emergency, that the best course of action initially will be for your client to go away and reflect on the situation in the light of the guidance and advice you have given him. It may be good strategy just to let time pass, to maintain the *status quo*, and to see how the situation develops. Always consider the option of doing nothing. Be very careful, however, to advise your client of any inherent risks, eg where there may be an alternative forum and where failure to commence proceedings or a delay in doing so may result in the other spouse commencing proceedings in a forum less advantageous to your client.

3.2.2 Referral

Depending on where you perceive your client to be in terms of dealing with a marriage breakdown, referral may be part of your strategy—(*see* Chapter 2, paras **2.3.7** and **2.3.8**).

3.2.3 Putting the onus on the client to take the first step

It is good practice, wherever possible, for your client to take the first step by speaking or writing to his spouse about the situation before the first solicitor's letter is sent. Make sure, however, that you plan such a course of action thoroughly with the client so that, for example, he knows exactly when the solicitor's letter will arrive and what it will say. Take care with the details, so that, for example, any such discussion takes place on a weekday when the other party can go straight to his own solicitor, rather than just before a weekend.

3.2.4 Getting the other party to a solicitor

It is helpful for all concerned if both parties are legally represented and you should consider with your client how best to encourage his spouse to contact a solicitor. A very simple first letter, referring merely to unspecified 'difficulties' between the parties and advising him/her to consult a solicitor will usually be the most appropriate. Avoid if possible making any references to such matters as financial disclosure which are more properly and effectively dealt with once the other spouse is legally represented.

3.2.5 Is it an emergency?

You may be faced at any stage in a case with circumstances which require you to consider acting with speed and without prior consultation with the other party or his solicitors, eg threatened abduction of children, domestic violence, dissipation of family assets. Emergency proceedings, while undoubtedly appropriate in certain cases, carry with them particular difficulties and dangers which must be explained carefully to the client before proceedings are commenced. The client may benefit in the short term from the injunctive relief obtained, but the anger and ill-will inevitably generated by such an application may create considerable difficulties in the future when other issues have to be dealt with. You will have to check the facts and assess the situation very carefully before advising that your client's position is serious enough to justify an application for injunctive relief, especially if an *ex parte* application is envisaged, weighing up the need to ensure that your client's immediate interests are protected against your duty to protect your client's best interests long term, which will include not raising the emotional temperature more than is necessary. This is particularly important where children are involved. Listen carefully to what your client has to say about his/her spouse—there may be a tendency to exaggerate the likelihood of trouble—but watch out for recurring themes which may indicate a real danger. You will need to be sure that your client understands not only the legal consequences of injunctive relief and that it is liable to be expensive, but also the likely emotional reaction of the person against whom the injunction is obtained and the longer-term implications of that reaction for the case.

3.3   Costs

3.3.1   Cost effectiveness

The importance of constant attention to the cost effectiveness of the strategy you propose, whatever the financial circumstances of the client, cannot be over-emphasised. As each step in the case is considered you must weigh the cost against the likely result of that action. The financial circumstances of your client may not permit you to deal with the case in the manner you would ideally have chosen, particularly if your client is legally aided and often in those cases where you represent a wife in financial proceedings. It is easy when dealing with financial applications on behalf of a wife to get immersed in the process of discovery and in obtaining a wealth of material while losing sight of the central issues in the search for the elusive and, in many instances, illusory Swiss bank account! Try thinking laterally about the issues rather than being bound by the linear approach imposed by the practicalities of discovery. You will have to tailor your strategy to fit the financial restraints imposed on it and ensure that your client understands and agrees the approach you are adopting.

3.3.2   Costs as part of strategy

The costs of the case, and in particular the costs liable to be incurred in the future, are an important aspect of strategy in any case, and especially in a case which may proceed to a defended hearing or be otherwise protracted. Awareness of the mounting costs of both parties creates an incentive to negotiate, particularly when one bears in mind that the costs of a hearing (including the preparation for it) may represent as much as two thirds of the total costs of a case. The importance therefore of making a *Calderbank* offer (*Calderbank* v *Calderbank* [1976] Fam 93) in financial proceedings is widely recognised by solicitors, but you may need to spell out the implications of not doing so to a litigious-minded client. (*See further* in Chapter 4, para **4.7.4**). The costs argument is one that can be used effectively with your own client to encourage a constructive approach to settlement whether the case is privately funded or the client is legally aided.

3.4 Personalities

3.4.1 The difficult solicitor

While the personality of the other solicitor will have some bearing on the strategy you apply to a particular case, you should not allow yourself to be dominated by it. Try not to worry your client by emphasising that the solicitor on the other side has a reputation for being difficult. You will do better to explain to your client that this particular solicitor takes a different approach from the one you would choose to adopt yourself and that you will have to plan your strategy accordingly.

The intransigent solicitor

Your strategy for dealing with an intransigent solicitor who appears unreasonable and unprepared, for example, to negotiate, may involve four-handed meetings so that the other party can see that your client's solicitor is reasonable and that his is not. Another way may be to by-pass the difficult solicitor by using counsel to negotiate. Make sure also that the pace of proceedings is maintained so that if negotiations fail the case can brought before the court without delay.

The aggressive solicitor

It can be very intimidating to be faced with an aggressive solicitor. The temptation will be to answer in kind. Avoid this at all costs. Try charm—it is much more difficult to be aggressive towards someone who is being pleasant to you than to someone who is being aggressive—this applies particularly at meetings, but likewise also with correspondence.

If you receive an aggressive letter, answer it firmly, but politely. It may be sensible to wait for 24 hours before replying to it, or to make a point of showing it and your reply to a colleague to ensure that you do not overreact. You may find that a point made against you in an aggressive manner is in any event a bad point. Do not allow yourself to be put on the defensive. Do not forget that if someone is being excessively combative, you can always produce a bundle of correspondence to the court. Tell your client a judge will not be impressed by aggressive correspondence and that in a discretionary area such as family law, it can be important and can colour the case to the other client's disadvantage.

It will help if you can recognise that aggressive letters or voluminous correspondence are a way of applying pressure on you and your client and forcing you into a defensive strategy. It is important to be able to resist being drawn in and to feel able to advise your client that the best thing to do is simply to resist responding in kind. This is most unlikely to prejudice his position and more often than not will have the effect of moving matters forward. Indicate to the other solicitor that you do not consider that the correspondence is assisting the case and that you reserve the right to deal with any of the issues raised at a later stage if appropriate. For your own part, always consider whether it is absolutely necessary to deal with a matter immediately in correspondence. Where, for instance, issues arise out of contact visits, it may be appropriate to advise your client to keep a diary rather than raising each relatively minor point at the time.

3.4.2　The difficult 'other party'

The character of the other spouse can have a great impact on your strategic planning and you should attempt to obtain a clear idea of his psychological profile from your client at the earliest opportunity.

A useful strategy in a case where the client's spouse appears to be acting unreasonably is to give his solicitor the ammunition to use with his client to produce the solutions you both feel appropriate.

3.4.3 The other party acting in person

Remain cool, calm and collected! It is prudent always in your first letter to advise a party acting in person to see a solicitor—this will be in your client's interests as well as his own. Be careful to explain matters, but not to advise him. Write clear letters in plain English and avoid the use of technical language which may be difficult for the layman to understand. Remember that he may at some time in the future consult and show your correspondence to a solicitor. Do not allow yourself to be side-tracked down any irrelevant paths of action.

In certain cases, it may be prudent to take protective measures against the risk of violence when meeting with the other party in person, eg by having another member of your department present at the meeting, or using a room with a panic button.

3.5 Commencement of proceedings

3.5.1 General considerations

Before commencing any proceedings, consider carefully all the consequences of so doing and be sure to advise the client accordingly. Once proceedings are commenced the case to some extent takes on its own momentum, but on the other hand the client has the ability to use the proceedings to exert control on the pace of the case if it appears that progress is slow. For example, explain to the client before filing a divorce petition that once the petition is filed it may not be possible to prevent the dissolution of the marriage before finances are resolved, but that once there are proceedings on the file, the court has power to make orders for discovery and to make a final order if settlement cannot be reached. Bear in mind also that the court has no power until *decree nisi* to make a variety of orders and in particular capital and transfer of property orders. For other considerations before filing divorce petition, *see* Chapter 9.

If there are any children, an application to the Child Support Agency will have an impact on strategic planning. Make sure that you have all the relevant information from your client at the earliest opportunity—*see* Chapter 2, para **2.3.3**. *See also* Chapter 8, para **8.6**.

3.5.2 Where to commence proceedings

Apart from matters of law which may dictate a particular jurisdiction or forum there are also practical considerations of cost and convenience to yourself and to your client to be borne in mind. It may help your client to feel more at ease if the case is being dealt with on home territory or at least neutral territory. It can be helpful to you as solicitor to be before a tribunal with which you are familiar.

Where there are potential alternative foreign jurisdictions the following considerations should be borne in mind:

(a) You must establish at the outset whether the English court in fact has jurisdiction to deal with the matter, remembering the different criteria required to establish jurisdiction for divorce, financial applications and cases involving children.

(b) Even if the English court has jurisdiction you must also ascertain whether there is another jurisdiction available which may give your client a better result.

Do not assume that the results of proceedings are likely to be the same wherever the proceedings are commenced. There can be substantial differences which may either cause an alternative jurisdiction to be more favourable to your client or quite the reverse. The golden rule is not to assume that what applies in England and Wales applies anywhere else. It is difficult but important to remember this throughout the case and at the most basic levels. Do not be chauvinist about the system you are most familiar with and do not rule out the possibility that what would happen elsewhere might just possibly be in your client's better interests!

(c) Remember that the jurisdictional requirements in other countries will not be the same as those used to establish English jurisdiction. In a case involving a child, for instance, the age of the child may be relevant. In some jurisdictions, eg in France, land will be treated in accordance with the law of the country in which it is situated.

(d) It is also very important to bear in mind the practical aspects involved in bringing proceedings in a different country. Cost and convenience to the client are significant considerations. Consider the availability of legal aid in this country where appropriate, and alternatives abroad (if available at all).

(e) Where there is a choice of jurisdiction and a clear advantage to your client in commencing proceedings in one jurisdiction rather than another, it may be necessary to act quickly to commence proceedings and establish jurisdiction before opening a dialogue with the other party and his advisers. This may apply where there is a pre-marital agreement which may be binding in one jurisdiction but not in another. The same applies in cases with children, and is particularly important if you are acting for a mother where the alternative jurisdiction may be one in which women have fewer rights by operation of law in relation to children than those they enjoy under English law.

(f) It is vital to get expert advice at an early stage from a lawyer specialising in the appropriate area of law in the other jurisdiction. You should advise your client of the need to make enquiries to ascertain whether the likely outcome of proceedings in that jurisdiction would be more advantageous, but be careful about the responsibility for costs. As to instructing foreign lawyers, *see below*, para **3.8.3**.

3.5.3   Form of proceedings

Think carefully also of the consequences of the form in which proceedings are issued (*see* Chapters 7 to 9 dealing with specific areas). There may be little point in obtaining a 'good' order for your client if any relationship of goodwill is destroyed in the process (*see* for example filing a petition, Chapter 9, para **9.1**, and effect of commencing injunctive proceedings, para **3.2.5** *above*).

3.6   Pace and timing

3.6.1   Client's emotional state

Bear in mind the client's emotional state, as already advised.

3.6.2   Maintaining the *status quo*

In some cases it may be in your client's best interests to maintain the *status quo* for as long as possible, eg in residence or contact applications under the Children Act 1989, or in certain financial applications, such as occupying the matrimonial home or preserving payment of certain expenditure.

3.6.3 Pace of proceedings

Bear in mind that whereas proceedings once commenced impose a structure and timetable upon a case, it may still, depending on your client's viewpoint, appear to be a very long time before a hearing is finally reached. It is very important therefore that without appearing to be aggressive you ensure that proceedings are commenced at a suitably early stage in the case. There will be exceptions to this rule, eg where a client wishes to conclude a financial settlement before divorce proceedings are commenced, but this will be possible only if the other party is also willing to deal with the matter in this way.

3.6.4 Timing of offers in financial applications

Think carefully about the timing of offers, particularly with regard to costs. For example:
(a) If you are acting for a husband who wishes to achieve an early settlement, consider making a *Calderbank* offer at the same time as early voluntary disclosure.
(b) If you are acting for a wife and you believe that her husband's disclosure may be less than complete, consider serving a detailed financial questionnaire together with proposals for settlement. The threat of extra costs which would be incurred in answering the questionnaire may act as a spur to achieve settlement.
   (*See also* Chapter 4, para **4.3** on the question of disclosure.)

3.7 Bringing in counsel

Most cases will not require counsel. You must have the client's agreement to instruct counsel and you should bear in mind that clients are increasingly unwilling to pay for what may seem to them like duplication of work, which may also make it harder for you to justify your own fees.

Whether you will need to involve counsel will depend on the weight and complexity of the matter, whether the case will proceed to litigation, your own experience and whether you are confident that you know what you are doing. It can sometimes be very useful if your client is unwilling to accept the advice you have given to reinforce it with a fresh view—counsel's Opinion. An hour spent in conference with counsel can give an opportunity for the client to hear his case reviewed and analysed in a way which is not always feasible for the solicitor dealing with it on a day-to-day basis, and can be useful to the solicitor in terms of persuading the client as to the way forward.

Do not forget that the quality of counsel's advice will depend on the quality of the instructions he is given. Be concise and do not enclose a heap of unsorted documents; give counsel time to consider what you have sent him. Remember that counsel may also be a source of referrals of new work.

As to choosing the right counsel for the job, ask other experienced solicitors for recommendations, keep to the counsel you know and to recommendations of the clerk of that counsel. Do not be fobbed off.

For instructing counsel in legal aid cases, *see* Chapter 10, para **10.5.2**.

3.8   Other experts

3.8.1   Accountants, financial, tax and pensions advisers, valuers

. *Choosing an expert*

Expert advice can often be useful in limiting the issues between the parties and a successful choice of expert can be an important element in your strategy. Particular care should be taken to ensure that the expert who is not familiar with matters of family law is properly instructed as to what is required of him and that those instructions are followed. Be sure that you and your client have a clear idea before instructions are accepted of the cost involved.

Client's own accountant

Your client's own accountant will be a helpful source of information as to your client's affairs, but he may not be the best person to give expert evidence, if for example a company has to be valued, by virtue of being too partisan.

Instructing an expert

Where possible the expert should be instructed jointly by both parties. Even if each side appoints his own expert, exchange statements and it may still be possible for the two of them to reach agreement.

The initial letter of instruction is very important. Make sure that you have made clear what you are asking for and that it will be acceptable to both parties, eg asking for an open market valuation as defined by the RICS. A specimen letter can be found in Appendix 5. Information you may need concerning insurance policies and pensions may often be obtained from the issuing body or you may need to refer to an actuary or pensions expert. The Law Society's Family Law Committee has produced a helpful form of letter of instruction to an actuary to value pension interests together with a questionnaire for use under FPR 2.63 which is to be found in Appendix 6.

As to instructing experts in legal aid cases, *see* Chapter 10, para **10.5.2**.

Costs

Be sure that you and your client have a clear idea before instructions are accepted of the cost involved. Make sure that it is absolutely clear from the letter of instruction who is responsible for payment of the expert's fees. If it is your firm, make sure that you are in funds to do so before the instructions are given.

For valuation of a business, including a farming business, *see* Chapter 8, para **8.1.8**.

3.8.2 Medical experts, psychiatrists and psychologists

When dealing with matters involving children, remember that the child must not be examined or any court papers disclosed to an expert without the leave of the court. Be aware of the different specialities and differences of approach, particularly within psychology and make sure that you find the right person to give the advice you need, and preferably someone with court experience.

If you have difficulty in finding a suitable expert, the Children Panel Administrator can put you in touch with a child care practitioner in your area who may be able to help. Alternatively, try your local child guidance clinic. Counsel may also have some suggestions. Make sure that your letter of instruction is clear and gives sufficient information. Do not forget to obtain your client's signature to a letter of authority where appropriate.

3.8.3 Foreign law experts

It is very important that advice on foreign law comes from an expert practising in the relevant field, rather than, for example your client's company lawyer abroad. The lawyer should by preference be English speaking. If your firm has not yet built up a database of such contacts, try the secretary of the International Academy of Matrimonial Lawyers (*see* Appendix 4).

It is prudent to write to the foreign lawyer yourself, setting out the facts of the case and detailing the issues on which you seek advice rather than merely sending the client and relying on him to explain the situation. Alternatively, you yourself may wish the client to instruct the foreign lawyer (to avoid finding yourself liable in costs or for wrong advice) but asking that the lawyer liaise with you. A legal aid certificate will usually cover the costs of taking advice from a foreign lawyer or other expert on jurisdictional and other issues arising in a case here.

3.9   Using private detectives and tape recordings

It is only in very rare cases that you should consider using any such methods, and it would be prudent to take counsel's advice before doing so. It is likely that if you are having to resort to such lengths, the case will go to court and you will need counsel to be able to justify your action.

Be conscious also that someone may be trying to eavesdrop on your telephone conversations with your client if your client and the other party are still living in the same house.

3.10   Reviewing strategy

You will need to review your strategy with your client regularly as the case proceeds. Be flexible in approach and prepared to change course when necessary.

4 Negotiation

4 Negotiation

4.1 Advantages of a negotiated settlement

It is important to remember that the court imposes a duty upon the parties and their legal advisers to negotiate: *Gojkovic* v *Gojkovic (No 2)* [1991] 3 WLR 621 at 636:

> 'It is incumbent on both parties to negotiate if possible and at least to make the attempt to settle the case.'

A refusal to negotiate may be reflected in the final order for costs and the same may apply if there has been a failure to make an offer or a counter-offer in good time. In the majority of cases where parties are legally aided and there are insufficient assets properly to meet the needs of both parties the question of who pays costs is still valid because of the statutory charge. In addition research has shown that those agreements reached through negotiation by the parties themselves are more likely to be successfully implemented than those imposed by the court. This is especially the case if they are negotiated at a time when both parties are receptive to negotiation rather than, say, at the door of the court when there is a greater likelihood of one or other or indeed both parties feeling pressurised into terms of settlement which they later regret.

Remind your client that the majority of family law cases do settle and reassure him that although you may refer to the court's approach to a particular issue or to what the court would be likely to decide in the client's case as you give your advice, you intend to ensure if possible that his case is concluded by negotiation rather than by a decision imposed by the court after a hearing.

A negotiated settlement is likely to achieve a considerable saving in costs, time and anxiety for all concerned.

4.2 The time to negotiate

4.2.1 Negotiation as a continuing process

Negotiation should be seen as a continuous process throughout the duration of the case. It may be helpful to look upon your prime role as that of negotiator for your client. Everything that you do for the client, including each step of the proceedings, should be treated as part of the process of negotiation. It is tempting to compartmentalise different aspects of the case rather than to look at the process as a whole, particularly when dealing with formal matters such as an affidavit of means, but you should endeavour to use each step as a means of advancing the case.

It is essential to establish the tone of negotiation both with your client and with the other solicitor at the very outset of the case. Bear in mind that different issues may be negotiated at different stages.

4.2.2 The state of mind of the parties

There are certain important matters that will need to be addressed carefully before any step in the negotiating process is taken. One that has already been mentioned in previous chapters is the state of mind of both parties. A settlement is likely to be successfully negotiated when both parties are willing to reach agreement, and a degree of sensitivity to the state of mind of the other party may assist you to put forward proposals at a time when they are more likely to be accepted or at the very least given careful consideration. This is of particular importance if the parties are to negotiate themselves at any stage (*see below*, para **4.6.4**). Be conscious too, of any particular stages in a case where you have negotiating power and make use of it.

4.2.3 Discovery

See below, para **4.3**.

4.2.4 Fiscal considerations

When negotiating a financial settlement it is important not to overlook the fiscal implications which may have a bearing on the timing of negotiations. It may be in the interests of your client or of both parties to implement an agreement or transfer an asset before a certain date (*see also* Chapter 8, para **8.7**). Avoidance of a potential tax liability (note particularly CGT) falling on either party will prevent the reduction of the amount available to divide between them and will benefit both parties.

4.2.5   New personal relationships

You may also need to look carefully at the development of other personal relationships both on the part of your client and the other spouse. If it seems likely that your own client may develop another relationship at an early stage, it may be worth attempting to settle the case at an early opportunity; conversely if it seems likely that the other spouse may be forming a new relationship it may be worth waiting until that is established. It need hardly be said that this sort of consideration must be handled with tact and delicacy and is unlikely to be the overriding consideration in the negotiating process. (For effect on financial provision *see* Chapter 8, para **8.1.3**.)

4.3   The rationale of discovery

Another crucial consideration will be the extent of your knowledge at a given moment. Without sufficient knowledge you are in no position to negotiate on any issue. The question of how much information you need in order to advise your client and to conduct negotiations on his behalf is always a difficult one, particularly in financial applications, and is inextricably bound up with the question of costs.

There is a great deal of concern amongst solicitors and the judiciary about cost effectiveness in family law proceedings and in particular in the area of discovery. While the solicitor is under a duty properly to investigate the other party's financial circumstances, the cost of pursuing particular lines of enquiry can far outweigh the ultimate benefit to the client. Anxiety has been expressed about the waste of time, energy and money that is sometimes incurred in pursuing an investigation into a party's financial circumstances, in extreme cases to the extent that there are insufficient resources left at the end of the day to meet the parties' needs. The issue is addressed in the following extract from the guidelines set out in *Evans* v *Evans* [1990] 2 All ER 147, *sub nom Practice Note* [1990] 1 WLR 575, para 11 which states:

> 'The desirability of reaching a settlement should be borne in mind throughout the proceedings. While it is necessary for the legal advisers to have sufficient knowledge of the financial situation of both parties before advising their client on a proposed settlement, the necessity to make further inquiries must

always be balanced by a consideration of what they are realistically likely to achieve and the increased costs which are likely to be incurred by making them.'

This will always be a matter for careful judgement and will depend in part on how much you and your client believe the other client is to be trusted.

The difficulty should not arise in a case where there are *prima facie* sufficient assets for a wife to receive an award which will satisfy the reasonable needs requirement (*see* Chapter 8, para **8.1.1**). It is most likely to be a problem in those cases where the parties want a clean break and any agreement or award will be final. It is then particulary tempting to ensure that every last asset is revealed and accurately evaluated. Indeed, if your client's application is to be properly adjudicated or compromised, it is essential that there should be full and frank disclosure of the other party's assets. The dilemma for the solicitor can be great, particularly when acting for a client who is convinced that there is a hidden crock of gold to be uncovered. On the one hand the practitioner risks incurring the wrath of the client if he does not pursue every line of enquiry to seek for it, on the other he faces the possible wrath of the court for allowing costs to be built up unnecessarily if the quest proves unsuccessful.

If you are in doubt as to whether to pursue a particular line of enquiry it may be helpful to try to form a judgement of the character of the other party untrammelled by the emotional overlay your client's description may involve. For example, the mere fact that the other party lives extravagantly does not mean that he is wealthy; he may be a spendthrift who lives from day to day without any substantial resources behind him. In many cases your client will probably be the best person to help you. In any event it is most important that you should discuss the issue with him, particularly if further substantial costs are likely to be incurred in the pursuit of the enquiry. If your client believes his spouse to be basically honest then it will probably not be worth doing so. For your own protection, however, you should seek confirmation from your client in response to a clear letter from you setting out the pros and cons of further enquiry. It is unlikely to be worth pursuing a matter which goes to the client's credibility over a relatively minor issue only and does not reveal hidden funds, as the court is unlikely to give great weight to such a point.

If you doubt your client's perception of the case, point out the costs implication of pursuing a particular course of enquiry, giving as accurate an estimate as you can of the costs which will accrue and making sure that the client is fully aware of the extent of the financial risk involved, including the risk of having to pay part of the other party's costs.

You must be sure that your client understands the extent of his entitlement to information and is prepared in the appropriate case to accept more limited discovery for the sake of achieving a reasonable settlement and that he instructs you accordingly. There will be cases where you feel able to advise your client that a settlement may be negotiated on the basis of voluntary disclosure, but you must be sure that the client understands that your advice is based on your experience and on a pragmatic weighing up of the additional costs that might be incurred in pursuing further discovery against the benefits of an early settlement.

4.4 Interaction between proceedings and negotiations

The desire to conclude a negotiated settlement should not preclude you from commencing proceedings and pursuing them in tandem with the negotiations (*see* Chapter 5, para **5.1**). It is indeed essential that you should do so in the majority of cases for a number of reasons. If proceedings are not pending at the time of a breakdown in negotiations, lengthy delays may ensue if you then have to start proceedings. Furthermore, this may permit the other party to commence proceedings themselves in a jurisdiction or forum which serves the other client's interests better than your client's. The very fact that proceedings are pending can add muscle to the negotiation, and this is particularly true as the hearing date approaches. The costs involved in a contested hearing are a powerful incentive to settle a case. Bear in mind that brief fees may be payable several weeks before the hearing and it may be appropriate to let the other solicitor know when you intend to deliver your brief so that negotiations can take place before this.

Where there are issues regarding children as well as financial issues, eg an issue as to where the children are to live which will have an effect on financial settlement, there are additional problems in dovetailing negotiations to proceedings.

4.5   Preparing to negotiate

4.5.1 Preparing the case

Formal negotiation will only prove successful if it is well-prepared and the parameters clearly drawn. You will need to agree with your client what he wants to achieve (*see* Chapter 2, para **2.3.4**), to ascertain as far as possible the other spouse's wishes, to establish the common ground between the parties which will then provide a foundation for building an agreement, to prioritise the issues that are not agreed, and to establish with the client the limits to which you may negotiate. It is also helpful before negotiation to build up a clear idea of the personality of the client's spouse and indeed of the other solicitor.

If the negotiations are to take place at a meeting make sure that you are clear in your own mind beforehand as to the purpose of the meeting and that you have a clear agenda, even if it is not a formal one. You may intend to use the occasion for the purpose of information gathering as well as negotiation. In those circumstances it is advisable to deal with the information gathering first.

4.5.2   Preparing the client

Preparing your client for the process of negotiation will be an on-going exercise. It will in many cases involve a degree of patience. You will need to explain the ritual of negotiation to the client unfamiliar with the process. Explain for instance that whatever proposal you make first will inevitably be interpreted as an opening bid.

If you are acting for a client who has considerable experience of business negotiation, it may also be advisable to explain to him the very real difference in family proceedings in terms of negotiating style and technique resulting from the emotional backdrop against which the negotiations take place. At the same time, however, you must stress that in terms of the actual result of settlement or any judgement given by the court, issues of emotion have no role to play and that there is no element of 'damages' in the court's award.

If your client is to be present at a negotiating session, be careful to explain the line you propose to take, eg that being pleasant to the other solicitor and client does not mean you are abandoning your client's position. Reassure your client that you are his representative with his interests at heart.

It will be helpful to your client if you can explain the dynamics of the meeting to him by describing the seating arrangements (eg all at one table or clients in separate rooms and solicitors together) and deciding who is to say what—the client must feel he is to contribute to the meeting rather than remain an onlooker, to have his or her say in the negotiating process. You may wish to agree a fall back position prior to the meeting. It is also prudent to accustom the client to the idea that he cannot expect necessarily to get everything he asks for, and that it may not be possible to reach agreement on all issues at one meeting

4.6 Forms of negotiation and their relative merits

Negotiations may take a variety of forms and the choice will depend to a large extent on the issues involved, the personalities (clients and solicitors), what stage in proceedings has been reached, and your own preference, depending on personality and experience.

Always be sure that you are clear as to whether you or the other solicitor are speaking openly or 'without prejudice'.

Try to think yourself into the other solicitor's and into the other client's shoes and consider what their reaction is likely to be to a particular proposal.

4.6.1 Between solicitors

Whether this is through correspondence, at a meeting, or by telephone will be a matter of choice dependent on the various criteria referred to above. In many cases you will combine more than one form, for instance by setting out proposals in writing and then following this up with a telephone conversation. A telephone conversation will by its very nature be less rigid than a letter and the ability to discuss and talk round an issue may enable solutions to be found to apparently irreconcilable differences.

However, meetings between solicitors in person tend to be more productive, especially if they are held at an early stage in the proceedings.

In an atmosphere where a conciliatory approach is to be encouraged the less experienced solicitor may be in danger of being 'seduced' to some degree by the charm, gentle flattery and persuasiveness of the other solicitor and, in a desire to please his professional counterpart, of losing sight of his objectives and his duty towards his own client. While it is helpful to your client's case that you should be on good terms with the solicitor for the other party, this is something to guard against. While the meeting will appear to run very smoothly, you may subsequently discover that you have given away more than you intended in an effort to 'please' the other solicitor.

If you are faced with a humourless negotiator who becomes over-identified with his own client's problems, you will need to distract him from his over-involvement, for example by the use of your own humour or by digression into other unrelated matters.

Similarly, an impassive negotiator who refuses to be drawn into a discussion but merely agrees to take instructions from a client is likely to cause you difficulty. Recognise the sense of unease that you feel in these circumstances and act appropriately. In some instances it may be necessary to help the other negotiator to relax. One solicitor is rumoured to have carried a packet of jelly babies in his pocket for this purpose—even the most difficult and pompous solicitor will find it hard to be difficult and pompous with a jelly baby in his mouth!

4.6.2 Four-handed meeting

A meeting between solicitors with clients present and participating can be a very efficient method of resolving a dispute, but be warned that it is difficult and exhausting! It has the particular advantage that the client has heard all that has been said and has had an opportunity to participate. There can be no suggestion subsequently of misunderstanding. Be careful, however,—it is a form of negotiation that can easily get out of hand. It can only be successful if you and your client are sufficiently confident in one another and in your negotiating skills and if all parties involved are keen to achieve a settlement. It is essential to have agreed the parameters of your intended settlement and not to be shifted from them in the heat of the moment. You must reserve the right to reach a settlement conditional on an opportunity to reflect overnight.

It can be helpful to arrange such a meeting if the other solicitor seems to be causing difficulties and to use it as an opportunity to illustrate this to the other client, or in effect to by-pass the other solicitor and to speak directly to the other client.

Set ground rules beforehand, eg that no-one is to be interrupted while speaking, that each party should be free during the meeting to go out of the room to talk privately to his solicitor (make sure other rooms are available for this purpose) and have refreshments available—meetings can be lengthy. Agree to disagree on some issues if discussions are going nowhere, rather than jeopardising an agreement on remaining issues. Following the meeting, send a letter to the other solicitor summarising the issues agreed or those to be concentrated upon.

4.6.3   Using counsel

Using counsel in negotiations can be helpful in exceptional circumstances where you are having particular difficulties either with the other solicitor or with your own client, who for example is reluctant to accept your advice. Remember, however, that counsel must be extremely carefully instructed as to the terms your client is prepared to accept and that involving counsel significantly increases the costs.

One option is the six-handed meeting at which both clients, their respective solicitors and counsel are all present. Counsel will normally prefer not to take part in round table negotiations but to move between the parties and their solicitors who will be in separate rooms.

Counsel may also be useful in negotiation to attempt to break a deadlock, eg when a matter has been fixed for hearing and counsel instructed, it may be useful to ask counsel to ascertain from the other party's counsel why that party is not prepared to settle. This information can then be fed into your correspondence with the other solicitor in an effort to advance the possibility of settlement in a manner which can subsequently be put before the court if necessary.

4.6.4   Between clients

The option of advising your client to negotiate directly with his spouse at any stage in the case is one that requires very careful consideration. While it can sometimes be used with great success it may also be very dangerous. It is an option to use sparingly and only when you are confident that the parties are negotiating from positions of equal strength. For example, a husband at an early stage in the case, when he is perhaps feeling guilty about the breakdown of the marriage, may offer a generous sum which his wife may reject, seeing it purely as an opening bid, whereas the husband is in fact being more generous than he will be later. It is generally better to advise clients not to discuss financial matters at an early stage because it can lead to badly crossed wires and increased bitterness. On the other hand it may be helpful to suggest they try to agree less contentious issues such as expenditure or suitable alternative housing. A visit by a husband to prospective new homes for the wife and children can be a very beneficial exercise. (In such a case make sure, however, that the wife is happy with the arrangement and that she does not see it as an attempt by the husband to retain control over her future life.)

4.6.5 Third parties

In some cases third parties may be able to assist in the negotiating process. In child disputes, for instance, a sister, aunt or grandparents may be able to encourage a more reasonable attitude or a satisfactory compromise. However, beware of the additional emotional overlays that may sometimes be present. Similarly, it may occasionally be helpful if other experts representing the parties, for example in financial proceedings, are encouraged to negotiate to narrow issues, if not to settle them.

4.7 Making an offer in financial proceedings

As already stated, it is essential that in all cases the question of making an offer and negotiating a settlement is tackled as early as possible following suitable disclosure (*see* Chapter 3, para **3.6.4**. and Chapter 5, para **5.5**).

4.7.2 Structuring the offer

Whatever form the offer is to take, it is important that it should be carefully structured and supported by a reasoned, if brief, resumé of the factors you consider the court would take into account and its likely decision. Bearing in mind that a letter of offer is very likely to be copied to the other client, give some thought to addressing the issues in a manner likely to appeal to the other client. It can be helpful to construct a practical scenario, eg based on proposed rehousing, rather than merely setting out bald figures. It is useful to separate the terms of proposal in summary form at some stage in the letter for ease of reference, particularly should the terms need to be drawn to the judge's attention at a subsequent hearing.

4.7.2 Open offer

Open offers are less common than 'without prejudice' offers, although the court has indicated that they are to be encouraged (*E* v *E* (*Financial Provision*) [1989] FCR 591, [1990] 2 FLR 233). Making an open offer whether in correspondence or in your client's affidavit will put considerable pressure on the other party. Bear in mind, however, that your client will never do better nor be able to go back on the offer unless circumstances change significantly. If your client receives an open offer it should be given the most careful consideration.

4.7.3 'Without prejudice' offer

You may wish to consider a 'without prejudice' offer as opposed to a *Calderbank* offer, for example at an early stage where there may not have been full disclosure or when your client is particularly anxious to make a proposal that you do not consider to be reasonable and which you would prefer not to form part of the *Calderbank* correspondence.

4.7.4 *Calderbank* offer

A *Calderbank* offer is a 'without prejudice' offer which expressly states that it may be brought to the attention of the court on any issue as to costs at the conclusion of the matter. In theory therefore it puts the recipient of the offer at risk as to payment of his/her own costs and possibly also the other party's costs from the date the offer is made if the final award is no more, or is less than the offer made. To be effective as a *Calderbank* offer the letter must make reference to costs and there must have been full and frank disclosure by both parties of all their respective financial and personal circumstances.

In practice, however, for purely economic reasons there is often a significant difference between the theory of *Calderbank* and the likely result if the matter comes before the court. In the majority of cases the funds in question will at best be barely sufficient properly to provide for the needs of both parties and there will be no opportunity for the court to impose the 'penalty' of a costs order. It is rare for a wife to be ordered to make a contribution towards her husband's costs.

That said, the *Calderbank* offer remains an important negotiating tool and a useful element in negotiating strategy, particularly in a case in which you are acting for a husband and the wife and her advisers appear to be taking an intransigent line and incurring considerable costs in the process.

It is crucial to stress, and this may need to be emphasised to the client, the importance of making a reasonable offer that you can respectably justify. Remember to set the letter out in such a way as to make the terms of offer easy to refer to a judge.

When you receive a *Calderbank* offer on your client's behalf it is important that you answer it promptly and constructively, dealing with each point that is raised. As with your response to any proposal which is unacceptable to your client, you should analyse the terms of offer carefully in order to ascertain where false assumptions have been made which can then be pointed out to the other party. Remember also that your client is under an obligation to set out counter proposals. Keep track of *Calderbank* correspondence on the file (perhaps by coloured tagging).

4.7.5 Drafting a consent order

Once agreement is reached you will need to draft a consent order. For general advice, *see* Chapter 8, para **8.13**.

4.8 Negotiating child related issues

Much of what has been already stated applies. It is most important to ensure that negotiations remain child centred. Unlike financial negotiations you are seeking to achieve a result which must be in the best interests of the *child* and the client may need to be reminded of this. It is sometimes very easy to slide into discussions which focus on the needs of the parents rather than the child. Be aware of this and constantly check that you are on the right track. Do not assume that you can negotiate matters relating to children on a 'without prejudice' basis.

You will need to be able to think laterally to come up with constructive ideas to unblock impasses that arise. Remember too that parents will have to communicate with each other in the future and that it is important that they should each be able to have their say in the negotiations rather than feel that the decision making process has been taken out of their hands. Four-handed meetings are useful, but be sure that you are able to contain the strong emotions which may be aroused.

Make sure that all proposals are very specific and practical and try to concentrate on what you are trying to achieve from a substantive point of view without worrying about whether for example a residence or a residence/contact order will be required. Be sure however that you are fully aware of the range of orders the court can make, and the criteria for each one, to achieve the best results. Bear in mind that certain orders have 'threshold criteria' (eg supervision orders) and others carry certain rights which can easily be overlooked (eg a residence order to a member of the extended family carries parental responsibility with it which natural parents may need to be reminded of). Make sure that your client understands the full implications of any proposals he wishes to make. This is of particular importance when your client is a parent seeking a residence order. While it may sound attractive in theory, does the client really want all the problems of daily care rather than 'quality time' at weekends, bearing in mind that the other parent may well be granted contact every weekend?

Underlying any negotiation will be the 'no order' principle set out in CA 1989, s 1(5) which states that the court should be certain before making an order that to do so is better for the child than making no order. If arrangements for children can be agreed it may be sufficient to record these in open correspondence (this can be a more flexible model as well). Any application, agreed or not, will have to persuade the court that an order is required so that at the end of a successful negotiation it is useful to ask oneself the question—is an order necessary?

Take care to keep issues relating to contact and residence separate from financial issues at all stages. It is usually appropriate to write two separate letters.

4.9   Other techniques

4.9.1   Lateral thinking

Where negotiations appear to have reached a stalemate whether during a meeting or otherwise, always endeavour to think laterally about the issues and to get round difficulties by producing an alternative suggestion which achieves the same objective by a different route. In some instances it may be useful to make a proposal which you know will not in itself be acceptable but which may serve to break a deadlock. A child centred lateral suggestion will be difficult to resist.

4.9.2   Brinkmanship

The brinkmanship approach to negotiation requires a considerable amount of skill and can be dangerous. You must be aware of the pace of negotiation and be very clear where you are on that scale. You must also clarify with your client where the 'brink' lies. While it has its role to play in certain instances such as towards the end of a case, when the issues are narrowed or when a court hearing is looming, negotiation by brinkmanship is not generally speaking an appropriate technique in family matters nor a particularly successful one.

4.10   Developing negotiating skills

The importance of acquiring and developing good negotiating skills cannot be over-emphasised. You will achieve this principally by watching others and by learning from your own successes and failures. Do not try to learn and put into practice every skill at once; some take longer to master than others.

4.11   When to stop negotiating

Negotiation is a continuing process and you should endeavour to continue to negotiate right up to a hearing. It can be dangerous to state categorically that what you have proposed is your client's final offer because this suggests an unwillingness to negotiate. You might, however, wish to state that your offer is not put forward as a basis for negotiation but because you consider it to be a fair and reasonable proposal.

There will be occasions when you have to stop negotiating, when to continue would put you in danger of going beyond the parameters of what you believe your client to be entitled to. You will not be acting in your client's best interests if you compromise merely in order to avoid a hearing. Do not be carried along by a feeling that you must settle at all costs. Sometimes it may be necessary to litigate even if it is expensive for the client. Be sure, however, that your client of modest means understands if he does litigate in financial proceedings what there may be to divide at the end of the day.

It is worth bearing in mind that there are certain areas of family law where negotiation is inappropriate and where your aim will be to bring the matter to court at the earliest opportunity. These include abduction, sexual abuse, violence, matters where a client is unable to give instructions, and cases in which disclosure is patently unsatisfactory. You may be able to negotiate later about other issues.

5 Litigation

5 Litigation

5.1 Proceedings as a framework for negotiation

It is important not to look upon proceedings merely as a process likely to culminate in a hearing at which a judge decides the outcome of
a dispute between the parties. In many family law matters, proceedings will be necessary to achieve a legally binding resolution to
the dispute between the parties, eg decree absolute or a financial
order, even if the issues are agreed and the order obtained by consent. Proceedings should thus be seen as a framework and a back-
bone to the negotiating process, and providing you make clear to the
other party's solicitor that you are using them in this way and that
your client remains open to any proposals for settlement, the commencement of proceedings need not be seen as aggressive (*see also*
Chapter 4, para **4.4**).

In some instances commencement of proceedings will encourage
negotiation. For example, a client may not be prepared to negotiate
a financial settlement until divorce proceedings are commenced
because there is no obligation to negotiate over capital save in the
context of a divorce. In other cases commencement of proceedings
will be inevitable, eg if there is a refusal to provide any financial support or refusal to accept that the marriage has broken down. Issuing
proceedings will show you mean business, but beware of starting a
cycle of cross-applications and aggression and never lose sight of the
need continually to look for opportunities to negotiate.

Once proceedings have begun, they can be used as a means of
obtaining information in an orderly fashion and ensuring effective
disclosure. Time limits and formal requirements will assist in maintaining momentum and imposing a discipline. Various stages in the
proceedings may be used as tools in the negotiating process, eg using
the 'threat' of a production appointment in cases where information
has been requested but not provided.

Be careful, however, that the goodwill generated by a continuing
negotiation does not lull you into a false sense of security which may
distract you from specific time limits and procedural requirements

laid down by the court, eg making your client's financial claims before her re-marriage, applications before decree absolute in respect of the matrimonial home, or filing answers and cross-petitions within the appropriate time limits. If necessary, negotiate and agree extensions with the other party's solicitor. Technically, extensions of time limits in Children Act 1989 proceedings require the leave of the court but if agreed between the parties often this can be done by letter to the court.

Once proceedings are under way, pay careful attention to their progress. It is dangerous simply to wait passively for the other party to respond. In order to help you to keep the initiative, it is useful to have relevant dates for the expiry of the other party's time limits as well as your own clearly marked in your diary.

While it may be important to maintain momentum, it may not necessarily be appropriate to pursue the proceedings with too much haste; there is a danger in concentrating on the procedural steps and overlooking the issues. Do not lose sight of the desired result—a negotiated settlement in which your client feels in control of the process and the outcome.

It is also necessary to recognise that there will be some cases which, for a variety of reasons, are unlikely to settle. Sometimes the particular psychological make-up of a client may preclude him from reaching an agreement, even through legal advisers. Once this becomes apparent the focus should be on the proceedings in order not to waste costs on fruitless negotiation.

5.2   Games solicitors may play

Be aware that you may come across solicitors who 'play games' with the litigation process in order to exert pressure on someone that they may see as less experienced, eg endorsing penal notices on orders, obtaining short time limits for the answering of long financial questionnaires, taking technical or 'clever' points, such as insisting on orders for costs on an indemnity basis. It is difficult to do much about it except to avoid joining in. If you feel under unwarranted attack, write short, polite and purely factual letters giving an account of each instance as it arises, and noting in conclusion that you reserve the right to draw your letter to the court's attention when the issue of costs comes to be decided. Take comfort from the fact that if the case does come to court, the judge will not be impressed by tactics which in effect amount to an abuse of the court process.

5.3 Guidelines in ancillary relief applications

Two helpful sets of guidelines have been issued concerning preparations for ancillary relief applications. These are the Practice Note issued following *Evans* v *Evans* [1990] 2 All ER 147, *sub nom Practice Note* [1990] 1 WLR 575 and *Guidelines for use by Solicitors in the Conduct of Ancillary Relief Claims* published by the Law Society. Both are to be found at Appendix 7 and deserve to be studied carefully. They have been prepared in the light of widespread concern over expenditure of unnecessary costs and the disproportionate amount of the family assets used up in this way.

5.4 Preparing affidavits and statements

5.4.1 Drafting generally

Beware of being too verbose or too brief. Try to balance the need not to make the affidavit too long and risking losing the sympathy of the court against the importance of not missing anything out. Keep it low key, not strident or opinionated and as far as possible in your client's voice.

Avoid archaic or legalistic terms such as 'motor vehicle', 'the said . . .', 'hereinbefore mentioned'. Consider how to refer to the other party, perhaps as 'my husband', 'my former husband', or 'Mr. Smith' rather than 'the petitioner' etc. In cases involving children it is advisable to use 'the mother' and 'the father'. This will avoid confusion where the party may be 'petitioner' in one set of proceedings and 'respondent' in another.

Strictly speaking the affidavit should contain fact and not argument, but as the affidavit should be seen also as part of the negotiation process, it is important to phrase your facts with that in mind. It is very difficult to distinguish between the two in child cases where you will use the statement to put your client's case and facts alone will be insufficient.

In child-related cases it is often helpful to commit your client's story to paper in the form of a statement at the earliest opportunity. The story may otherwise be liable to change as it is told to various others involved, such as a court welfare officer. In taking the statement take care not to induce your client to present too colourful a picture because he thinks this is what you want and/or need. Test the story carefully as you go through. Expressions such as 'never' and 'always' in describing behaviour need to be treated with particular circumspection.

Generally, the presentation of facts should go to support your client's case, but avoid the temptation to select facts as representative which on closer examination may be exceptional. If you consider that your client's case has areas of weakness it may be prudent to deal with them head-on in the affidavit in order to avoid the client being put on the defensive in the witness box. By the same token do not exaggerate the alleged faults of your client's partner and remember that your client's view of these is unlikely to be as impartial as the judge's view will be. Reference to the areas of concern rather than graphic description of instances of past behaviour presents a more measured approach and one which can be developed, rather than retreated from, at the court hearing.

5.4.2 Affidavits of means

It is helpful to prepare an affidavit of means from a checklist or precedent, as it is easy otherwise to overlook items such as the parties' dates of birth, that need to be included. It is also helpful to use the details provided by the client in answering a memorandum of financial information (*see* Appendix 2) as the basis of the affidavit.

5.5 Discovery

5.5.1 Extent of discovery in financial applications

Refer to Chapter 4, para **4.3**.

Where there are assets outside the jurisdiction there are methods of tracing them, including under The Hague Convention, but always bear in mind the help a good foreign lawyer can provide and above all the cost involved.

5.5.2 Serving a questionnaire

Be reasonable and restrained in your requests. Focus on the issues and remember the potential cost of producing the documents you are requesting. The content of a questionnaire is so dependent on the particular case that it is not recommended you should use a standard form of questionnaire, nor delegate the task to someone with little knowledge of the file and issues involved. It may be useful to have a list of potential questions at your side, such as from Longman's *Matrimonial Precedents*, to help with phrasing particular enquiries; but even then, think carefully and modify each question to suit the particular case.

The most useful information that you are likely to elicit will come from very specific questions arising from the material that has been disclosed so far. You may only have been given an old set of company accounts but instead of just asking for more recent accounts, read what you have been given carefully and analytically, so that precise questions can be put which demand a precise answer and cannot be evaded.

When looking at the replies provided, be aware not only of the information they contain, but also of what information is missing, eg if there is no indication in bank statements of the funding of a family holiday, there may be an overseas account or payment by a foreign contact.

5.5.3 Answering a questionnaire

If it is not unduly onerous to your client to answer a question in a questionnaire, advise him to answer it, even if you feel that the scope of the question goes further than a court might have ordered. Failure to answer is likely to be construed as implying there is something to hide. If the request is excessive, then supply what you consider to be relevant and sufficient, putting yourself in the position of the other solicitor, explaining that only material which falls within this head is being provided.

Be careful of agreeing to an order that your client answer a questionnaire within a specific time period. You may be thinking of the order as just specifying the time you have to get down to tackling the questionnaire whereas in fact you are agreeing to provide all the information and documents sought. If you want to argue that certain questions should not be answered do not agree to blanket orders of this sort.

5.5.4 Production appointments

Production appointments can be very useful if handled properly. They are helpful in negotiation in that they allow sight of information at an earlier stage in the proceedings which formerly could only be obtained at the hearing itself. It may be helpful, for example, to see bank files, mortgage application forms or to require a new spouse to produce information as to his means. If you strongly suspect that your client is being told one story and the bank manager another, requiring the bank's files to include internal memoranda of meetings might of itself trigger proposals to settle above the level presently being put to your client.

Beware, however, of the costs involved; it can be very expensive to obtain documents from banks and the expense may at the end of the day be borne by your client.

5.5.5   Privileged documents and statements—difficult areas

Correspondence and documents belonging to the other party

A letter passing between the other solicitor and his client is privileged. If such a letter inadvertently comes into your or your client's possession, it should be promptly returned to the other party's solicitor. It is acceptable to advise your client to examine any documents relating to the other party's financial affairs to which he has open access, although you should be cautious as there has been judicial criticism of photocopying or examining privileged documents. The client should not open sealed correspondence or break locks in order to gain sight of a document. You should advise your client to keep his own papers where they cannot be found by the other spouse.

Valuations

Your client is under a duty to disclose any valuation in his possession, even though he is not relying on it (*Chand* v *Chand* (1979) 9 Fam Law 84, CA).

Medical and psychiatric reports

For consideration of the duty to disclose reports in child cases, *see* Chapter 7, para **7.1.3**.

It is good practice always to check with your client that the medical report is accurate before sending a copy medical report to the other party.

Documents produced by a guardian ad litem to his own solicitor

A guardian has access to a wide variety of privileged documents by virtue of his role. Care must be taken in dealing with confidential information which should not be passed on to other parties. For example you may receive from a guardian details from a social worker's file which are intended for you only.

Statements made during mediation

See Chapter 6, para **6.4**.

The Law Society's Ethics and Guidance Department will answer queries on such matters (tel 071–242 1222)

5.6 Pre-trial review

A pre-trial review should be treated seriously and looked upon as an opportunity at the very least to narrow the issues and at best to achieve a settlement. With this in mind it is important to prepare your case thoroughly, not forgetting to have current costs figures available, and it is worth taking your client with you to the appointment and checking that the other solicitor will be doing the same.

5.7 Witnesses

5.7.1 Expert witnesses

Matters to be considered when instructing expert witnesses are dealt with in Chapter 3, para **3.8**.

5.7.2 Witnesses in financial applications

It will be rare in financial cases to be calling witnesses of fact other than expert witnesses and in any event you will be unlikely to do so unless a hearing is imminent. Family and friends do not tend to make impressive witnesses in financial cases. Financial conduct is rarely in issue and even then corroborative evidence from other witnesses is hardly ever required.

5.7.3 Witnesses in other proceedings

In a domestic violence or ouster application or in the rarer event of a defended divorce you will need witnesses as to fact. In the former case this may include police officers and neighbours. Medical reports will usually be accepted as agreed without the need to call the witness.

In a child related case there may be a large number of potential witnesses as to your client's character, abilities as a parent, etc. You will need to be careful to choose the most objective witnesses and to focus on the important issues. When you receive from the other party a number of 'character' statements you will need to consider carefully which you intend to test by calling for cross-examination. It may be better to accept their evidence rather than to allow the judge to see and hear impressive witnesses for the other side.

If you need to call witnesses to appear at a hearing remember that some may need a witness summons to show to their employer, eg police, teachers, health visitors, or where they refuse to attend voluntarily—do not leave service until the last minute. You should check that they will come to the hearing; it is dangerous merely to rely on them to turn up. Take care, too, to explain what the procedure will be, and the fact that if they give a statement they may have to attend court. Persuasion may be needed to encourage potential witnesses and to ensure that they feel comfortable and at ease about giving evidence, and are not hoodwinked into it.

5.7.4 Child as witness

There are various methods of getting a child's evidence before the court and as a general rule you should try to avoid calling a child as witness if at all possible. The court does not in general look favourably on the production of child witnesses and only in very rare cases will it be in your client's interests to do so. Where possible, agree a statement with the other party, or consider whether you can put the necessary information before the court in another form, eg included in the welfare officer's report, or given by a third party (hearsay evidence is admissible—*see* Chapter 7, para **7.6.1**).

If a child has to give evidence, you should endeavour to protect him as far as possible, perhaps by the use of screens and agreeing limited issues of questioning in advance with the other party. Aggressive cross-examination of a child witness should be avoided at all costs.

5.7.5 Interpreters

Make sure that if an interpreter is required you find an official interpreter, who has court experience. It is not a good idea to use anyone
who is connected with your client. Check where appropriate that he
speaks the right dialect of the language concerned. The Law Society
Legal Practice Directorate holds a list of interpreters, as do the
Institute of Translation and Interpreters (tel 071–713 7600) and The
Association of Police and Court Interpreters (tel 0732 451700).

5.8 Preparing client and witnesses for hearing

This is an important aspect of preparation for any hearing.
Remember that the hearing will be an intimidating experience for the
client. It will be helpful to anyone unfamiliar with the court process
for you to explain procedure, and to describe the layout of the court.
Some clients may not realise, for example, that a hearing may take
place around a table and that they will be sitting opposite their former spouse, whereas others will be reassured to learn that the court-
room is much less formal than they had expected. Some clients may
need tactful guidance as to what they should wear for the hearing.

You will need to explain the process of giving evidence and you
should try to prepare your client for the sort of questions he is likely to be asked. Advise your client to answer the question but not to
elaborate, and in particular not to criticise the other party gratu-
itously in the witness box. Do not underestimate the stressful nature
of the experience of giving evidence. You should explain to your client
that while he is on oath you will not be able to discuss any matters
relating to the case with him; it may be disconcerting for a client otherwise to discover that you are unwilling to discuss the case over the
lunch break!

The same process of preparation applies also to witnesses.

5.9 Counsel

5.9.1 Do I need to brief counsel?

The question of whether counsel is briefed for a hearing will depend
on a number of matters, including your own proficiency as an

advocate, the level of court, whether it will be cost efficient to do so, and what your client can afford. There are also other valid reasons for instructing counsel, such as to obtain the benefit of an objective view of the case.

In a child-related case you may consider that the detailed knowledge of the case you have acquired cannot easily or effectively be transferred to counsel. On the other hand you should instruct counsel if there is a danger that you are becoming over-involved in the case—these cases will probably seem the hardest to hand over! Where you are acting in care proceedings for a child on the instructions of a 'guardian ad litem' you will be expected to appear yourself, and particularly at a final hearing. If you are a member of the Children Panel you will have given an undertaking to do so.

Practice will also vary from firm to firm and in different parts of the country. For example whereas many solicitors will appear at the hearing of interim applications at the Divorce Registry, few will appear at a final hearing. There is a growing tendency for solicitors to appear in child hearings in the higher courts.

Remember that you need your client's authority before instructing counsel. If counsel is instructed on a final hearing it will be helpful to have a conference with counsel well before the hearing.

If you do your own advocacy, you need to ensure that you have proper backup in court to fulfil the role you as solicitor would otherwise play, including taking notes and organising the papers. This can make the choice of solicitor as advocate a more expensive option than briefing counsel. In a legal aid matter you will not receive legal aid for anyone to be present at the hearing other than the advocate solicitor. You must take a commercial view of this. If the case is complex and will involve extensive cross-examination over a number of days, it may be worth arguing on taxation that the cost of a clerk or a trainee solicitor was necessary. You must also be aware of the disruption to your other work if you intend to embark on a hearing lasting several days.

5.9.2 Preparing the brief

Be thorough but use your discretion and do not send counsel every last sheet of paper on your file. If you have already sent counsel detailed 'Instructions' your brief may not need to be lengthy. Similarly if the documents enclosed with the brief itself are detailed the brief itself need not be a huge document. While you should not deliver the brief earlier than necessary, make sure that you leave counsel sufficient time after the delivery of the brief properly to prepare the case. Remember that the date of delivery of briefs can be a huge pressure point for settlement. Bear in mind, however, that this is less relevant in legal aid cases where counsel is paid for work done rather than on delivery of the brief.

5.9.3 Negotiating fees

This can cause difficulties for an inexperienced solicitor as counsel's clerks are generally tough negotiators. It is helpful if you can use the same set of chambers regularly so that a good working relationship develops. With experience you will learn to recognise the appropriate rate for a particular counsel on a particular type of case.

Your negotiations with counsel's clerk may concern not only quantum but also when the fee is payable. Some chambers now operate a system of structured payment which involves early delivery of the brief, eg four weeks before the hearing, when a percentage of the fee is payable. Thereafter should the case be settled and the brief cancelled, only a further appropriate part of the fee is payable, depending on how close the cancellation is to the hearing. This has the advantage of enabling you to deliver briefs in reasonable time for counsel to prepare the case rather than waiting until the last moment before delivery in an effort to settle the case and avoid counsel's fees.

Remember that the brief has to be marked before the hearing so that you cannot reduce it afterwards as a hidden contingency.

In legal aid matters there is no need to agree counsel's fees before a hearing, but the brief should be marked 'Legal Aid' with the certificate number and date of issue.

5.10 Documents to produce to the court

5.10.1 Agreed court bundles

Check with counsel, if instructed, which documents he wishes included. Make sure that agreeing the bundles is not left until the last minute, and that it is properly done with clear and correct pagination. Check that all documents copied are clean, with no hand-written comments in the margins for example. Keep 'without preju-dice' and open correspondence separate and make sure that you also have a separate *Calderbank* correspondence bundle ready. All the correspondence should be in chronological order with the most recent piece at the back, rather than file order. Prepare an index and use dividers so that documents can be found easily. Make sure there are a sufficient number of bundles for those attending. The preparation of the bundles is likely to be a delegated task and you must ensure that it is properly supervised, not least because you will be the one who wants the floor to open and swallow you up when the court finds the pagination goes awry or a crucial page has been illegibly copied. It is good practice to deliver one bundle to court and another to coun-sel for the other party in advance of the hearing.

While it is unnecessary to include all correspondence and docu-ments in the agreed bundles, make sure that you take everything with you to court so that something you originally considered to be of no significance can be produced should the need arise.

5.10.2 Other documents

In ancillary relief applications these will include a chronology of rel-evant facts (*see* guidelines in *Evans* v *Evans*, Appendix 7) which will normally be prepared by counsel, an agreed statement of assets and liabilities, marking those not agreed, and a costs estimate. The lat-ter is a most important document. Make sure that it is up to date and is a realistic assessment of costs being incurred during the hearing itself. Set out the estimated costs broken down for each day that the hearing is scheduled to last.

In child-related proceedings it is helpful to prepare an agreed statement of facts, a chronology and a family tree if appropriate.

5.11 Solicitor's role at hearing

5.11.1 Attendance

In legal aid cases a solicitor will not be present at a hearing where counsel has been instructed and usually a clerk will sit with counsel and the client.

If your client is not legally aided and funds allow it, your attendance at the hearing may be helpful. As well as assisting counsel in
preparing the necessary papers and note taking etc, you may have
an important role to play in reassuring your client, keeping your eyes
and ears open for what is happening in court on your side or the other
side and the judge's reactions—body language is important.
However, do explain the costs consequences to your client. You may
agree that you will 'top and tail'—attending before and after court
when negotiations are most likely, and when the case is being prepared and reviewed with counsel. If so, make time to attend the hearing for your client's own evidence and the judgement at least. You
must also ensure that your client has met and feels confident in the
person from your office who will be attending.

5.11.2 Door of the court settlements

If there are substantive negotiations at the door of the court there
may be intense pressure on your client to settle. If the settlement is
negotiated by you or on a counsel-to-counsel basis you will need to
ensure that it is indeed a fair one for your client, that your client does
not feel that he has been pressurised into agreement against his will
or better judgement, and that it is an agreement to which he freely
accedes and is fair; otherwise it may lead to subsequent unhappiness
with the settlement and difficulties with implementation. Make sure
that you explain the terms carefully and fully to your client and the
reasoning behind your advice that the terms are acceptable, particularly where the terms fall short of his expectations.

5.11.3 Conduct in court

Your conduct and indeed that of your client is particularly important
when you are in a small court. Be very careful what impression you
are making on the judge. You should be dressed neatly and not in a
manner to attract attention to yourself. Beware of theatrical ges-
tures, eg over vigorous shaking of the head or sharp intakes of breath
at particular statements made by the other party. Generally try to
avoid client's tears. In cases dwelling on distress or fear, such as
domestic violence, a degree of emotion may be helpful if genuine, but
broadly your client should be encouraged not to appear melo-
dramatic.

5.12 Advocacy

It is outside the scope of this book to deal in detail with the subject of advocacy. This is a skill which is learnt through experience, by watching others and by a suitable training course. Set out below are some general guidelines to keep in mind.

5.12.1 Preparation

Careful preparation is vital. You should plan the structure of your case in detail and it is helpful to prepare an opening speech even if you are not making one. Prepare an outline closing speech which you can modify as the case progresses. Prepare your questions for each witness, having a clear idea of what you want him to say. Be careful, however, not to over-prepare because you will need to be open to developments that are bound to arise during the course of the hearing.

It is very helpful to find out what you can about your tribunal in advance of the hearing. If the case is in a court with which you are unfamiliar it may be worth ringing a colleague in that area. Your arguments may have to be tailored to account for the particular views of a certain judge. Assess the formality expected and pitch the tone of your address accordingly. For example, in the family proceedings court, the hearing can be very informal and extensive legal argument should be addressed to the clerk rather than the bench or can in some cases be dealt with beforehand, whereas in the county court you can combine your final submission on the evidence with a legal submission to a district judge. In the High Court the hearing will be considerably more formal.

5.12.2 At the hearing

Do not rush into your opening before checking whether the judge has read the papers in the case—if the proceedings are emergency proceedings and he has done so there may be no need for you to say anything. Try to be aware of the impression you are creating on the judge. Be aware when a point is not being taken and move on to the next one—you may be able to come back to it again at a later stage in a different form. If the judge appears not to be listening, pause, or address him directly, or change the subject. Do not allow yourself to be hurried.

5.12.3 Examination and cross-examination

Write down evidence as it is being given and mark points for re-examination—different coloured pens are useful. Use a notebook rather than loose sheets of paper and write on one side of the paper only so that cross-examination material can be inserted. Make sure you can read your own writing and abbreviations.

If you are very familiar with your case and with the basic law, thinking on your feet should not be a difficulty. Strategies for dealing with unexpected evidence, so that you are not flustered or hurried by it, will come with experience. You will also develop a pattern and technique for cross-examination; it is helpful to have clearly in mind what you expect a witness to say. Be aware of when to stop and do not re-examine unless you have to.

As to the tone of cross-examination, keep it low-key but firm. Aggressive examination is rarely helpful and can be positively harmful to your case. You can however afford to be tougher with professional witnesses.

5.12.4 Final speech

It is very difficult to make a final speech as soon as you have finished cross-examination. Have your final speech prepared in outline in advance so that you can add any new and relevant information to it. Do not be afraid to ask for a few moments to prepare yourself should you need to—remember that the judge is also busy at this stage considering his judgement.

5.13 After the hearing

Be sure to explain the judgement carefully to the client. It is good practice also to set out the terms in a letter in language which the client can understand. Do not be hasty in making a decision to appeal, but on the other hand be aware of time limits which are very short.

Make sure practical details are clear, eg if there is a contact order, exactly when contact is to take place. If counsel is to draw up the order, be sure that all practical arrangements are dealt with satisfactorily. Watch in particular that costs are properly covered.

Finally, remember that the case is not over until the order is complied with and the costs paid!

6 Mediation

6 Mediation

Mediation in family law is an actively developing area and one of increasing importance, both as an attractive option for the client who wishes an amicable resolution of family difficulties and as a new area of work for the suitably trained family law practitioner. It is important therefore that the family law solicitor should be aware of the current position and of likely future developments.

6.1 What is mediation ?

Although the format and procedure of mediation in family disputes may vary, its essential feature is that it is a process aimed at assisting the parties involved to work out their own solutions to their differences themselves. It offers an alternative to litigation or negotiation.

The mediator's role is to facilitate this process. He does not offer advice or suggest solutions, but can clarify proposals and objections to them and can suggest what might make a proposal acceptable. Attention is concentrated on the future rather than on what has passed. The mediation can be comprehensive or can relate to a particular issue only. It is part of the mediator's role to ensure that each party has an equal opportunity in the process and that there is a power balance between the parties, and to manage the discussions.

The role of mediator is therefore quite different from that of the solicitor, whose responsibility it is to represent the interests of the party instructing him, even though adopting a conciliatory approach and encouraging his client to reach a settlement by negotiation.

The process is currently in a state of active development and change. Major pilot schemes and important research are in progress in an effort to establish the most appropriate models for mediation in the field of family law.

6.2   Distinguishing conciliation, mediation and reconciliation

There was formerly thought to be a clear distinction between conciliation and mediation services. Conciliation, either under the aus-
pices of court-based schemes or independent services affiliated to the
National Association of Mediation and Conciliation Services
(NAFMCS), formerly the National Family Conciliation Council
(NFCC), concentrated on the resolution of issues concerning children
and divorce generally, rather than financial matters. Mediation services were first offered by the Family Mediators Association (FMA),
which offers a comprehensive service, dealing with all aspects of the
breakdown of the marriage, including financial issues. NAFMCS is
now running its own pilot scheme to explore the provision of comprehensive mediation and the results are likely to be published in
the near future.

Independent conciliation or mediation has the advantage that the
process can be started prior to the commencement of proceedings and
its lack of formality is attractive. The limited availability of legal aid
funding is however a drawback—*see below*.

In terms of the essential aim of the facility offered, ie that the parties should work out their own decisions, the terms mediation and
conciliation are interchangeable and mediation is now the preferred
term. Both should be clearly distinguished from 'reconciliation', the
object of which is to explore the possibility of saving the relationship
and the marriage.

6.3   What services are available

There is at present no unified provision of mediation or conciliation
services across the country. The services in your area will be either
court-based or independently run schemes affiliated to NAFMCS or
operated by FMA.

6.3.1   Court-based schemes

For conciliation appointments in child cases, *see* Chapter 7, para
7.1.4.

Certain courts also now hold initial appointments in financial proceedings, although this is not widespread. A district judge explores, guides and directs the parties and their advisers through discussion in an informal setting. You should be careful to prepare yourself and your client properly for such an appointment. At best, important issues may be settled on such an occasion, and even if they are not, then at least they may have been narrowed.

6.3.2 NAFMCS

Over 50 services are affiliated to NAFMCS. Details of local services and further information can be obtained from the organisation (for address and telephone number, *see* Appendix 4).

All services operate within a code of practice agreed with the Law Society and the SFLA. The code relates primarily to disputes regarding children and divorce only, although it recognises that there may have to be consideration of finance and property issues where these cannot be separated. Such consideration is however restricted to preliminary discussion only, for example when it is necessary to decide where children are going to live.

Conciliators will normally have a background of social work training and may have further specialised conciliation training as well. Fees will vary according to the particular service, but most services offer a sliding scale or will waive fees for those unable to afford them. The only legal aid funding available for independent conciliation is limited to £29.50, which can be claimed as a disbursement in respect of a report from a NAFMCS service. Procedure will vary but the aim is to offer an opportunity to the parties to sit down together in an informal atmosphere to consider their difficulties in a constructive manner. A series of meetings may be necessary to resolve the issues.

NAFMCS has been operating a pilot scheme to provide comprehensive mediation in six different local services throughout the country, each using a different model of mediation. Some models have involved a lawyer trained as a mediator at some point in the process, but not necessarily present throughout. In each case, the client is recommended to instruct a solicitor as an independent adviser. Although the results of the pilot scheme have yet to be published, it seems certain that NAFMCS will in future provide comprehensive mediation and a lawyer mediator will probably be involved in some part of the process but not necessarily throughout.

6.3.3 FMA

The FMA has some 300 mediators, almost equally divided between those with a legal qualification and those with a family or social work qualification. It was set up in 1988 with the close co-operation of the Law Society Family Law Committee and SFLA and its code of practice is approved by them.

The FMA's mediation model is co-mediation whereby a legally trained mediator and a family (ie social work) trained mediator work together. The current practice is for them both to mediate throughout. Comprehensive mediation is offered, and clients may be referred at any stage in a separation either to explore the possibility of living apart or to deal with problems arising during or after separation or divorce. Mediators bring their knowledge and experience into the discussions but encourage the parties to work out their own solutions to their difficulties.

The co-mediators are specially trained by the FMA, which also operates a supervision and accreditation system. All mediators are covered by a block indemnity policy.

Usually three to six 90-minute sessions are required to reach an agreement, after which both parties are encouraged to take the proposals to their own solicitors to be converted into a formal settlement. The fees, which vary regionally, are usually divided three ways; to each of the two mediators and to cover the solicitor mediator's overheads as the meetings will normally take place in a room at his office. Legal aid is not available.

The FMA now offers the additional facility of a central referring service through the ADR Family Register. All the solicitor or client will need to do is to ring the freephone telephone number (listed in Appendix 4) to be put in touch with a mediator and co-mediator from the ADR Register after the appropriate referral discussions have taken place.

Alternatively contact FMA (address and telephone number in Appendix 4) for addresses of local mediators and further information.

6.3.4 Family Law Bar Association Scheme

The FLBA is revising its present scheme which is a form of arbitration whereby both solicitors submit agreed facts to a member of the

Bar for a fixed fee and receive an 'Opinion'. Details may be obtained from the secretary of the FLBA, Paul Coleridge QC, Queen Elizabeth Buildings, Temple, London EC4.

6.4   Confidentiality, disclosure and privilege

Both the mediation organisations understand that the success of a mediation depends upon full and frank disclosure. They each have detailed schedules of information which is required. Those schedules will be available with the summary of the mediation to the lawyer advising the client, either during the mediation or following its outcome. It is explained to the parties that disclosed documents are not privileged in any subsequent proceedings.

It is central to the mediation process that the parties involved should feel able to discuss their difficulties and possible solutions to them freely without the fear that what is said may subsequently be used in some manner against them should mediation fail and proceedings be commenced. For this reason the contents of discussions are confidential and privileged save in exceptional circumstances. This position was reinforced in the recent case of *Re D (Minors) (Conciliation: Privilege)* [1993] CA, where it was held that statements made by the parties in the course of an attempt to resolve their difficulties through mediation are not admissible as evidence except in very unusual cases where a statement is made clearly indicating that the maker of that statement has in the past caused or is likely to cause serious harm to the well-being of a child.

6.5   The solicitor's role

6.5.1   Referral

You should be familiar with the local services available and ready to explore with your client the possibility of mediation where appropriate. The SFLA actively encourages its members to promote mediation and provides information via its newsletter and seminars.

It is clear that the process of mediation will not suit every client or be appropriate in each case. Some cases will have to be determined by the court and in others the solicitors will be able to negotiate a satisfactory settlement. Mediation is a third alternative. There must be a willingness and degree of commitment from each party for there to be any chance of successful mediation. Where such commitment does exist, mediation can result in substantial savings of costs and may also give the clients the additional satisfaction of having settled their difficulties themselves. Even if the mediation is only partially successful, the solicitor subsequently instructed may build on the information obtained and the partial agreements reached.

Mediation also ensures proper use of a solicitor's time and expertise. It does not imply an abandonment of one's legal adviser, since it is part of the process that each party is strongly recommended to seek advice from his own solicitor during the mediation process or after it at any time he wishes.

If you consider that mediation may be appropriate you should discuss the possibility of referral with your client. You should explain to your client that mediation is not a substitute for legal advice.

The most convenient way of referring the client would be to use either FMA's leaflet, the ADR Register (*see above*, para **6.3.3**), or, if appropriate, the leaflet from your nearest NAFMCS service. This gives the relevant telephone numbers to call and also explains the nature of the process. Many clients who believe that mediation is appropriate will wish to discuss the possibility direct with their spouse. Sometimes, however, it may be sensible to raise the matter with the other spouse's solicitor to test out whether the suggestion will have his support and if not, to seek to establish why. Sometimes this may be because the solicitor is unfamiliar with the process of mediation or may even be hostile to it, but on other occasions the solicitor may feel that his client is not emotionally or temperamentally suited to the mediation route. There is no point in pressing mediation unless the process is a voluntary one, but the argument that until you have tried something you cannot tell whether or not it will work can be a sound one to present.

6.5.2 During and after mediation

The solicitor has a valuable complementary role to play alongside the mediation process. It is important that you keep in touch with your client and are ready to advise him at any stage, both as to factual matters and points which may not have been considered. It may also be necessary for you to alert the parties to any difficulties you become aware of during the process, for example if you do not consider that there has been adequate disclosure. Be careful, however, not to become involved in the mediation process itself.

Once the mediation is completed the mediation service will compile a report summarising whatever conclusion has been reached and recording the information upon which any agreement is based. The agreement may require proceedings to be commenced or continued to obtain a decree and/or a consent order.

It may happen that you are asked by a client to act upon an agreement reached during mediation where you consider that there are deficiencies in the agreement, perhaps because there has been insufficient disclosure. Ideally, your involvement during the process of negotiation will prevent such a situation occurring, but it may be that you are not instructed by the client until the mediation has been completed. You must advise the client of the deficiencies. If your client wishes to abide by the agreement then you should explain your reservations in writing and obtain written instructions to proceed. If on the other hand your client feels unable to abide by the agreement after receiving your advice, you should raise the matter at the earliest opportunity with the other party's solicitor. The agreement reached in mediation is not such as to make it binding. However, you will need to spell out in some detail the client's reservations about the agreement in order to justify the change of mind. This is obviously important from a negotiation point of view as the resiling from the agreement will undoubtedly anger the other party. Of course, the situation would be different if the agreement had been entered into formally by the parties on the basis of full disclosure and with legal advice. In those circumstances it would be a binding agreement and could only be variable on an application to the court in accordance with the *Edgar* principle (*Edgar* v *Edgar* [1980] 3 All ER 887).

6.5.3 The solicitor as mediator

You may wish to consider the possibility of qualifying as a mediator as a member of an established mediation service.

To become a member of FMA and an accredited mediator it is necessary to satisfy requirements as to professional qualifications and experience in practice (at least five years' post qualification and recent work including a substantial amount of matrimonial and family work), to complete the FMA's training in mediation, to be accepted by the Board of Management as a member, to complete a specified number of mediations with supervision and to satisfy accreditation requirements.

Accreditation to NAFMCS requires a similar process of selection and training, proven competence and work experience. For those without social work or Relate training selection is based on aptitude as well as relevant qualifications.

It is not currently possible for one solicitor to advise both parties whose interests may conflict and to attempt to do so may put the solicitor in breach of the Law Society Practice Rules. However, as part of the NAFMCS pilot scheme joint appointments are being offered at the Cambridge Family and Divorce Centre to couples contemplating divorce who wish to obtain information rather than legal advice about their legal position, how they may resolve their differences and the steps to be taken to obtain a divorce. A formal change in the rules in order to permit such appointments may follow.

It is now possible for a solicitor to offer mediation as part of his practice (*see* the Law Society's *Guide to the Professional Conduct of Solicitors* (6th edn)). Details of insurance, training and a code of practice will have to be considered. One obvious difficulty to be overcome by the individual solicitor who wishes to offer mediation as part of his practice is the question of fees. Most mediators currently work for modest hourly rates, while solicitors' offices have expensive overheads to meet. However, this is an area which the family law practitioner needs to keep in mind as an important opportunity for new work in the future.

7 Specific Areas 1—Children

7.1 Acting for a parent
    7.1.1   General considerations
    7.1.2   Seeing the child
    7.1.3   Duty to disclose information
    7.1.4   Conciliation appointment
    7.1.5   Contact with former spouse's partner
    7.1.6   Removal of a child permanently from the jurisdiction
7.2 Applications under Children Act 1989
    7.2.1   General considerations
    7.2.2   Parental responsibility
    7.2.3   Residence orders
    7.2.4   Family assistance orders
7.3 Acting for other members of the family
7.4 Acting for the child
    7.4.1   Generally
    7.4.2   Conduct of Litigation
    7.4.3   Personal relationship with client
7.5 Sexual abuse
    7.5.1   Generally
    7.5.2   Experts
    7.5.3   Level of court
7.6 Evidence
    7.6.1   Generally
    7.6.2   The child's wishes
7.7 Adoption and care proceedings
    7.7.1   Generally
    7.7.2   Step-parent adoptions
7.8 The Children Panel

7 Specific Areas 1—Children

7.1 Acting for a parent

7.1.1 General considerations

One of the most difficult aspects of dealing with any proceedings involving children is to persuade the parent who is your client that the child is not a weapon to be wielded in your client's personal battle with the other parent and that he must endeavour to look at the issue from the point of view of what is in the child's best interests. It may take several meetings before you are able to achieve this and it must be handled sensitively. It is very hard for those in the process of divorce or separation to accept that the other spouse remains just as much a parent of the child, and that parents are parents for ever.

As a solicitor it is necessary to separate the issues surrounding the children from the issues between the parents and to explain the importance of doing so to your client, while at the same time recognising that there is a fundamental dynamic of bargain between the clients which will underlie their discussions. Have your duty towards the child in mind when you are acting for the parent and remind your parent client that you have that duty.

7.1.2 Seeing the child

Your client may be very anxious for you to speak to the child yourself, but you should resist this. The child should not be involved in the litigation, except in appropriate cases, when if he has something important to say you can arrange for him to have an independent channel of communication—*see below*, para **7.4**. On the other hand you may find it helpful sometimes in forming your own view of the case to observe the children briefly and informally, for example if they have to accompany your client to a meeting. Recognise the limits of this observation, however.

If a child comes to see you of his own accord in connection with pending proceedings involving him, you should inform the other solicitor as soon as possible and send him a copy of your attendance

95

note if appropriate. If the child is mature enough to have come to see you of his own initiative, he deserves a courteous hearing. You must make it clear to the child at the outset that you are under a duty to inform your client and the other party of anything he says to you.

If the child wishes to speak to someone in confidence, then you must explain that he should not talk to you and that you can help him to find another solicitor, guardian, social worker, or conciliator with whom he can discuss the matter. If a court welfare officer or the Official Solicitor is already involved, he may be the appropriate person, otherwise if the child is older, we suggest you contact the Law Society Children Panel—it is advisable to discuss this very delicate situation with a colleague and you should notify the other side. Even if you are unable to make immediate arrangements you should try to agree a course of action enabling him to speak to someone as soon as possible.

7.1.3   Duty to disclose information

There will be occasions when your duty to the child conflicts with your instructions from your client. You may for example request information, which turns out to be prejudicial to your client's case—what should you do with it? This will inevitably be a difficult issue to resolve. Much will depend on the significance of the information obtained, but as a general rule it is good practice to disclose it while endeavouring to limit the damage it may cause as far as you can. In such cases it is very important that as far as possible you have alerted the client beforehand to the possibility that certain information you ask for may turn out to be detrimental to his case and that it is nevertheless your view that the information should be put before the court. The most common example of this is a psychiatric report obtained on a parent. At the time of writing it is not clearly established whether there is a duty to disclose but you may feel uncomfortable if you are in possession of a report indicating your client has serious difficulties which relate to parenting while maintaining an application for residence. If leave has had to be obtained from the court for the psychiatrist to see the court documents and the subsequent report is not disclosed, the other parent may very well *subpoena* the doctor in any event.

7.1.4 Conciliation appointment

Although conciliation is not currently a formal part of the legal process, certain courts have for some time run their own schemes to deal with child-related disputes and you should familiarise yourself with the procedures adopted at your local court. In-court conciliation services are provided by the court welfare service who on occasions liaise with local out-of-court services.

At the Principal Registry in London an in-court scheme is operated in all contested applications in child proceedings, including an application to vary an existing order. The parties and their legal advisers must attend the first appointment where the district judge will sit with a welfare officer and the appointment will be conducted informally with a view to ascertaining whether the case is suitable for conciliation. It is important that both clients and solicitors treat this appointment seriously. Where a conciliation service exists, the judge is required to consider, before ordering a welfare officer's report, whether the case is suitable for conciliation.

The role of court welfare officer as conciliator is distinct from his role when ordered by the court to prepare a report. In the former his role is as that of conciliator defined above; in the latter his duty is rather to assist the court to resolve disputes which the parties are unable to resolve themselves. If a conciliation attempt fails, then a report for use in the proceedings should be prepared by a separate welfare officer.

The Practice Direction dated 18 October 1991 (which applies to the Principal Registry only but may be adopted elsewhere) requires the parent with whom the child/children lives to bring all children over nine to the conciliation appointment. In extreme cases where, for example, you fear there may be violence or the child has not seen the other party for a lengthy period of time, you may consider it in the child's best interests to make arrangements for the child to be in a separate room or to apply to the court for leave not to bring the child to the initial conciliation appointment.

This is one occasion when you will come into contact with children during a case and it may be helpful to consider briefly your own demeanour towards the child. You should try to appear friendly, eg by shaking hands or making some other friendly contact with the other party and his solicitor, introducing yourself to the child who is living with your client and making light social conversation. You may also introduce him to the other client's solicitor. When the child is living with the other client a friendly 'hello' to the child and a handshake is probably sufficient.

If you are acting for the parent with whom the child lives, prepare him for the appointment by explaining what is likely to happen, who will be there, the layout of the room etc, and ask him to explain this to the child. Make it clear to the client that there may be a lengthy period of waiting before the appointment so that he can have with him the means to amuse the child during that time.

7.1.5 Contact with former spouse's partner

The 'other man' or 'other woman' will be a particularly difficult issue for your client and you may be asked whether it is reasonable for the child to have to come into contact with a parent's new partner during contact visits. If the relationship is one of long standing and is likely to be of a permanent nature, then you should advise your client that the court may well view this as something the child will have to become accustomed to, and that in the long term the court is unlikely to seek to prevent the child coming into contact with that person. If on the other hand the parents have only recently separated, the court may consider in the short term that the child should get used to seeing the parents separately before a further element is introduced.

If you act for the parent with the new partner you should advise him to adopt the softly softly approach and try to explain how confusing the new situation may be for the child.

7.1.6 Removal of a child permanently from the jurisdiction

Where there is a residence order or an old style custody order in force a child cannot be removed from the jurisdiction without the consent of every person who has parental responsibility for the child or the leave of the court. Do not underestimate what such an application will involve. It may be fiercely contested as it will almost inevitably substantially curtail the other party's contact with the child. Court decisions are very much on a knife edge, and even Court of Appeal decisions can go either way and apparently contradict conventions. It is therefore essential to prepare your client's case for such an application with great care, providing as much detailed evidence as possible of such matters as proposed housing arrangements and schooling.

7.2 Applications under Children Act 1989 (CA 1989)

7.2.1 General considerations

Proceedings should be specific and only when it is in the child's best interests for there to be proceedings. Remember that the court can make an order without an application in other family proceedings so that you should avoid cross-applications if possible.

Everything should be done to minimise the need for applications to the court if at all possible. Here you may find your skills put to the test. Encourage your client to consider and understand the concept of parental responsibility which underlines the legislation governing the court's involvement with children (CA 1989). Remind yourself and your client of the no order principle, that is that the court will not make an order unless it is better for the child than to make no order (CA 1989, s 1(5)), and of the welfare checklist (s 1(3)).

Although technically the court only has regard to the welfare checklist in private proceedings which are contested applications, it is a useful way to focus the client's mind on the relevant considerations to be made when deciding how to approach arrangements for children on the breakdown of the family.

Emphasise that the court will consider any applications regarding children to be wholly separate and apart from financial matters such as maintenance (now usually outside the scope of the court because of the Child Support Act 1991). Equally, in most cases the 'fault' leading to divorce (unless it relates to behaviour directly affecting the question of parenting) will be regarded as irrelevant. It is often hard for the parent whose spouse has committed adultery to accept that that parent's rights *vis à vis* the child are unaffected by that adultery. It is particularly important if there are to be court proceedings to tell your client that those proceedings are not to be discussed in detail with the children. It is crucial that the children involved do not feel they must take sides, or indeed emotionally support one parent or the other.

Beware of making gender assumptions in any application. Questions of practicality will be much more relevant. This applies also in cases where you are dealing with homosexual or transsexual parents, but these are much rarer and it is advisable in such instances to take advice from a more experienced colleague or from counsel. The Children's Panel now has a helpline for its members who are faced with difficulties and need advice.

The long-recognised principle that delay in hearing proceedings is prejudicial to the interests of the child is now enshrined in the Children Act (s 1(2)) and the court has power to draw up a timetable for the disposal of the case.

7.2.2 Parental responsibility

Acting for the unmarried father

Do not forget that the unmarried father does not have parental responsibility. This should be addressed particularly if the client father has been closely involved with the care of the children. Try to obtain agreement from the mother that a parental responsibility agreement be drawn up (use the prescribed form and register in the Principal Registry of the Family Division). However, remind the father that this is a responsibility, not a stick with which to beat the mother! Be conscious, too, of the importance of not depriving a father of his right to make an application, eg for residence or split residence, provided it is not a wholly unreasonable application. Bear in mind that it is a particularly difficult area in which to advise your client with certainty and the court's approach will vary, depending on the age of the children, the impression made by your client, and his approach to the litigation.

Advising the mother

When advising the mother of non-marital children on the question of a joint parental responsibility agreement, remember that if there is such an agreement any testamentary appointment of a guardian by the mother will not take effect until the death of the father unless there is a residence order in force in her favour.

The question of whether it is appropriate for a father to have parental responsibility is a difficult one. Some say it should follow more or less automatically while others take the view it has to be able to work in practice in order to be appropriate, for example where there are strongly differing views on religion it might not be appropriate.

7.2.3 Residence orders

In the context of domestic violence or other serious issues where the police are called to assist, the police will not remove a child who is not returned after a contact visit if the parent who has the child has parental responsibility, unless there is a residence order in favour of the other parent.

It is usually sufficient for a parent to have parental responsibility, rather than requiring a residence order, in order to be placed on the local authority housing list, but you should check this with your local authority.

For the significance of a residence order in child abduction cases, *see* Chapter 9, para **9.2.6**.

For joint residence orders in favour of a parent and step-parent, *see* para **7.7.2**

7.2.4 Family assistance orders

Such orders are only made in exceptional circumstances and cannot be applied for. However, they can be very helpful. The order provides for a probation officer or social worker from the local authority to befriend, advise or assist the child, his parent, or any person with whom the child is living or who has a contact order, for a period of six months. They are particularly useful in cases where a supervision order may have been applied for but the threshold criteria in CA 1989, s 31 cannot be met. The only criteria for making an order is that the circumstances are exceptional and all persons named in the order consent.

7.3 Acting for other members of the family

There are an increasing number of Children Act applications being made by members of the extended family, primarily grandparents but also aunts, uncles and others. Be wary of these applications being made simply to 'bolster' one or the other parent's case, and where there are genuine concerns it is usually appropriate to ensure the family members' application is kept distinct and separate from the parents'. Independent representation will be necessary. However, no such application should be made unless there are separate interests to be determined by the court (*Re M (Minors)* 14 October 1992, CA).

7.4 Acting for the child

7.4.1 Generally

Although still rare, there are an increasing number of children in private proceedings who are instructing solicitors themselves. A solicitor may be contacted by one of the solicitors for the parents or by the child himself. By either route the solicitor must satisfy himself at the outset whether in his view the child is sufficiently mature and has an understanding to entitle him to have his own representation without a 'guardian ad litem'. This may sound easy but can be very difficult. Try to assess from a general conversation with the child whether he is capable of identifying the nature of the dispute in which he finds himself and whether he understands the longer term consequences of the course of action he wishes to embark upon. It is with the 10–13 age group that it is particularly difficult to assess a child's capability, especially when the child may appear articulate and streetwise, but is emotionally damaged or not emotionally developed. You will have to decide whether such a child has the capacity fully to understand not only the practical, but also the emotional, implications of what he proposes.

If there are already experts such as child psychiatrists involved, it may be useful to seek their views but ultimately it is for the solicitor in the first instance, subject to any enquiry by the court (*see below*), to decide. Even if the child is not capable of giving his own instructions, it may still be appropriate for him to be independently represented. In private proceedings, this will usually be via the Official Solicitor who may ask that you continue to act for the child on his behalf if a relationship has developed between you. Alternatively on occasions a court welfare officer will take over this role (acting as guardian ad litem) and the solicitor will continue to act. It will probably be appropriate in these cases for proceedings to be transferred to the county or High Court (the Official Solicitor having no status in the family proceedings court). Remember that 'panel' guardians (ie those who are members of the various regional panels established under CA 1989, s 41(7)) will not get paid for work done in private proceedings as they are not specified proceedings under the Children Act (*see* s 41). Guardians' fees are not a disbursement which is covered by legal aid.

If the solicitor feels the child is sufficiently mature to instruct a solicitor direct, then an application will have to be made either to be joined as a party in existing proceedings or for leave to commence his own action. At an application for leave the court may enquire into the question of maturity and there have been a number of interesting and controversial decisions on this point. It is not an area for an inexperienced solicitor and advice and help should be sought either from more experienced colleagues or a member of the Children Panel.

7.4.2 Conduct of litigation

The same considerations apply when acting for a child as when acting for parents. If acting for a child direct, the duty to be clear and sensitive to the client is particularly high. Remember that the child may not be as developmentally mature as he appears and may need time and help to assimilate information which comes to light during the course of proceedings relating to his parents.

As with other clients remind the child on a regular basis that he may apply to withdraw his application or leave the litigation to continue between the adults.

It is always essential to explain clearly and carefully each step of the proceedings with some idea of the likely timetable. Young people often are not able to comprehend why issues cannot be dealt with immediately. Make sure that you attend all hearings yourself.

7.4.3 Personal relationship with client

The risk of developing too close a relationship with the child client is higher than with adult litigants. One's natural response is to protect and guide but it is important to keep within professional boundaries.

It is necessary to remember and to remind the child that your involvement in the child's life is transitory. As you near the end of the case, you should start drawing your relationship with your client to a close so that he is prepared for you to be no longer involved closely with him although accessible if future problems arise.

If you find yourself over-involved, speak to a colleague or seek the advice of a friendly guardian ad litem or social worker who may be able to suggest ways of disentangling yourself.

7.5 Sexual abuse

7.5.1 Generally

We have raised this specific topic as it is featuring more and more often in private proceedings and the media have highlighted cases where the allegation of sexual abuse has been made to thwart a father's contact/residence application. Whether acting for parent or child, be cautious. Do not make any assumptions about the truth or otherwise of the allegation. Sexual abuse happens in the 'nicest' of homes but on the other hand false allegations are undoubtedly made. Recognise your own emotional response to the allegations and take it into account.

If the allegation has been made directly to you (ie if acting for a child) know and act upon the standard child protection procedures issued by the Law Society and your own local authority. If you are unaware of these, contact the Law Society and your local Child Protection Team (usually based at the local police station).

If the allegation arises through the parent who is your client, you should notify the other solicitor in writing promptly, setting out the allegation in as even-handed a way as possible and suggesting a joint approach in relation to the investigation of the allegation in accordance with recognised child protection procedures. A reference should be made immediately to the local authority in which the child resides and the process should be explained to your client carefully and fully.

The raising of allegations of sexual abuse will heighten the emotional temperature of any proceedings like no other. It is not unusual (although extremely unfortunate) for solicitors to 'reflect' their particular clients' stance either by displaying outrage at an apparently unfounded allegation or over-zealous condemnation of the alleged perpetrator and his representative. *Any* allegation of however minor a nature should be investigated, using the proper procedures with appropriate safeguards put into place pending that investigation (ie supervised or suspended contact).

When acting for a father it is often the case that he will wish, understandably, to 'clear his name' through the proceedings. While the investigation of any allegation is important for the child, it is often the case that the outcome will be inconclusive and it is not the court's role to vindicate one or other adult's innocence. This is particularly difficult for many fathers who have been the subject of allegations to accept, but unless such a course is demonstrably in the child's interest, the court will not proceed to a finding of fact.

Whilst a civil court in dealing with an allegation of sexual abuse will still be applying the burden of proof appropriate to the civil courts, ie the balance of probabilities, it may be appropriate to remind your client that in the context of sexual abuse the courts have held that the probability must be very high (*Re G (A Minor) (Child Abuse: Standard of Proof)* [1987] 1 WLR 1461).

7.5.2 Experts

There is often a temptation when an allegation of sexual abuse has arisen, to 'swamp' a case with experts from both sides. By far the preferred course is to agree an expert (such as a child psychiatrist or a psychiatric social worker trained and experienced in the investigation of allegations of sexual abuse) to undertake an assessment which will of course involve interviewing the child. Leave will have to be given in these circumstances by the court and ideally any such report should be filed with the court and served on all parties. It is important that there be a joint instruction by the parents or that the expert be instructed by the child's representative if there is one. If after such a report has been filed, either of the parents are unhappy with it, the usual practice is then to seek 'paper' second opinions by other experts if felt appropriate. It will be only in the most exceptional case that the court will allow the child to be interviewed again and your client should be made aware of this at the outset. It is also not usual practice for there to be more than one expert involved in the initial interview—one hears occasionally of cases in which a father's solicitor asks that his psychiatrist be present at an interview being conducted by a psychiatrist instructed by the Official Solicitor. This is not good practice and it is likely the court would not think such a course was in the best interests of the child. It is essential to remember that no court documents can be shown to any expert (for a paper second opinion or otherwise) without the leave of the court.

7.5.3   Level of court

The Children (Allocation of Proceedings) Order 1991 is currently under review. Article 7 of the current order, which applies to public law proceedings, provides for the transfer up of a case involving conflicting evidence about the risks involved to a child's physical or moral well-being or about other matters relating to the child, and therefore applies to a case involving allegations of sexual abuse. Article 8 provides for private law proceedings to be transferred and it is likely that the court will expect a matter involving alleged sexual abuse to be dealt with either at the county court or High Court level. Certainly if there is going to be an extensive dispute of psychiatric evidence, it is appropriate to transfer the case upwards.

7.6   Evidence

7.6.1   Generally

By virtue of the Children (Admissibility of Hearsay Evidence) Order 1991 hearsay evidence is admissible in any proceedings concerning the welfare, maintenance or upbringing of a child. There has been some debate as to whether this covers only second-hand hearsay or whether it extends to third-hand and indeed more remote hearsay. The general view is that any hearsay evidence is admissible but obviously the more remote it becomes, the less weight will attach to it. It will therefore not be surprising to find statements filed which include various elements of hearsay. Whilst one should avoid hearsay evidence if at all possible, you are certainly not precluded from its use. However, caution should always be exercised in the drafting of statements not to include prejudicial hearsay which will simply inflame the litigation.

7.6.2   The child's wishes

Under the welfare checklist (CA 1989, s 1(3)) one of the matters to which the court must have regard is the ascertainable wishes of the child. If acting for a child direct (ie the child having maturity and understanding of the proceedings without a next friend or guardian ad litem) this will be quite straightforward. When a solicitor represents a very much younger child through a guardian ad litem, it will be for the guardian to ascertain the wishes of the child and obviously the amount of weight placed by the court on those wishes will to a very large extent depend upon the age of the child expressing them. However, as solicitor acting for the child, it is essential that those wishes are put to the court clearly and with the dignity and respect they deserve in all cases.

7.7   Adoption and care proceedings

7.7.1   Generally

A family law practitioner is likely from time to time to come across cases which involve such specialisms. It is beyond the scope of this book to deal with them here, but if you are faced with such matters you should tread very carefully and take advice from an expert.

7.7.2   Step-parent adoptions

In the private law sphere, the area of adoption work you are most likely to come across relates to step-parent adoptions. Courts have taken a differing view on the suitability of step-parent adoptions but the Court of Appeal generally has stated that such adoptions may not be appropriate, particularly if the natural parent with whom the child no longer lives is maintaining a relationship through contact or otherwise with the child. In the past, it has been felt more appropriate to apply for joint custody orders for the parent with whom the child is living and his or her new partner, rather than the making of an adoption order which fundamentally changes the legal basis upon which the child resides with his newly constituted family. In light of the Children Act, under which a natural parent has the right to apply for contact with a child even after an adoption order (but only with the leave of the court), there is some argument to suggest that the finality of an adoption order has been in any event eroded to a certain extent. If the child is old enough to know his absent parent and has a relationship with him or her, it is likely to be more appropriate for you to advise your clients to seek a joint residence order which will have the result of granting the step-parent parental responsibility for the duration of that order. Adoption law is currently under review and this section should be read in the light of any changes made to the Adoption Act 1976 in the future.

7.8 The Children Panel

The Children Panel (previously known as the Child Care Panel) is administered by the Law Society and recognises that work involving children requires expertise. To apply to be a member of the Panel a solicitor needs to have sufficient experience to demonstrate familiarity with the range of work commonly encountered in this field, to have been practising for at least three years, and to have completed an approved course on the CA 1989 covering law, procedure, skills and practice. An undertaking in relation to representing children under CA 1989 is also required. References will be sought from the clerks to the justices and guardians ad litem. There is an interview conducted by a Panel solicitor and a guardian ad litem based on a case study you will have been sent previously. You are then either admitted on to the Panel for a period of five years (fee of £120 plus VAT), deferred with recommendations for further training etc, or refused. Panel lists are widely circulated among family proceedings courts, guardians ad litem, local authorities, libraries etc.

8 Specific Areas 2—Financial Provision

8 Specific Areas 2—Financial Provision

In this chapter we have not sought to consider every aspect of financial provision, which would merit a long book to itself. Instead we have concentrated on issues which frequently present themselves and can cause difficulties for the less experienced practitioner. We have highlighted common problems, given information and advice and where appropriate referred to other useful works of reference. Standard texts are listed in Appendix 1.

8.1 Assessing quantum

8.1.1 General guidelines

Despite the wealth of reported case law on the subject, the Court of Appeal has repeatedly indicated that what matters most are the factors for consideration set out in Matrimonial Causes Act 1973, s 25 and the facts of the particular case.

Having said that, there are principles to bear in mind, the most important and helpful being the need to balance reasonable needs against available resources, and the need to consider the net effect of any proposed provision. Producing a proposed solution and testing it against the parties' needs and circumstances is, of course, never as easy as it sounds because of personalities, expectations etc. Two matters in particular are often sticking points: the quality of proposed housing and whether the former wife should be expected to return to work and for what remuneration. No two people's ideas of what is 'reasonable' are likely to be precisely the same, particularly when each will be materially affected by the outcome. Be aware, too, of the tribunal if the case is likely to come to court; different judges place different emphasis on such issues.

Nor is it always easy to work out how to deal with the facts themselves, eg when there are substantial pension rights, a family business or farm, a very long marriage or a very short marriage but where there are children. Reported cases can give some guidance but ultimately it is a case of trying to find a solution, often requiring imaginative thinking, which fits the resources and the requirements of this particular family.

8.1.2 Contribution

This commonly takes the form of contributing to the building up and/ or running of a family business, but also includes the contribution made by a parent who remains at home to raise a family. Both will have some significance, particularly where the contribution is exceptional (*see Gojkovic* v *Gojkovic* [1990] 2 All ER 84), but their importance should not be exaggerated; the consideration of present circumstances and reasonable needs will be a more important factor.

8.1.3 Conduct

Conduct is rarely taken into account in considering financial provision. It is most likely to have relevance exceptionally in short marriage cases. Even then, only conduct which has a bearing on the financial position is likely to be relevant, eg financial recklessness, a decision to remarry or cohabitation with another party (where party is receiving financial support from that party). The latter can be a source of grievance to a former wife who finds that the court is very interested in the financial circumstances of her new partner but pays little regard to those of her former husband's new girlfriend. As a matter of good practice, make sure that you are aware of any new relationship your client has formed and as far as possible whether the other party has done so (*see also* Chapter 4, para **4.2.5**). Remember the position may change during the course of the proceedings.

8.1.4 Pre-marital co-habitation

The case law suggests different approaches as to the importance to be attributed to this. As a general rule it should not be given too much weight, but is to be treated as a circumstance among others to be taken into account.

8.1.5 Pre-marital contracts

If the agreement was drawn up in the UK with the benefit of full disclosure and separate legal advice then its terms are likely to have a significant bearing on the financial provision made on divorce, particularly if the marriage has been short and circumstances have not varied significantly. It will not be binding on the court and will be one consideration amongst others. Generally, a foreign contract will carry less weight in proceedings here, not least because there is unlikely to have been full disclosure and separate legal advice.

8.1.6 Substantial assets

The size of assets available is a consideration, but even with long marriages the percentage the court will consider reasonable for the wife to receive will diminish in direct ratio to the size of the assets. Even in cases of extreme wealth the test of 'reasonable needs' will predominate, unless it can be shown that the wife has made an exceptional contribution (*Gojkovic* v *Gojkovic* [1990] 2 All ER 84).

8.1.7 Personal injury awards, compensation for loss of office and inheritances

Again, such sums will be treated as one of the factors to be taken into account. In an extreme case where, for example, a party receives a personal injury award in respect of injuries inflicted by the other party, such a sum will not be treated as part of the family assets to be divided. It is important to look at what the sum is intended for and to treat it appropriately, eg compensation for loss of office should not be treated as capital if it is intended as a substitute for lost income.

8.1.8 Treatment of a business in calculating quantum

In those cases where a party's interest in a business is the family's major income-producing asset, it is inappropriate to treat that interest as a capital asset, unless the business is a public company, or a sale of the company or a flotation is imminent. It may, however, be treated as an asset to be used as security to raise a loan for the payment of a lump sum. In any event it is likely that you will need to have at least a broad idea of the company's worth, and with practice and a basic understanding of share valuation you should in most cases be able to obtain this yourself from the company accounts.

Nevertheless, beware of matters such as property values. The FLBA publication *At A Glance* is helpful.

We have already commented on the importance of obtaining an accurate idea of the value of such assets while at the same time ensuring that the costs involved do not outweigh the benefits of so doing. Obtaining a professional valuation can be extremely expensive and may provoke the other party into obtaining one as well. Normally it should not be undertaken if it is clear that the company will not be sold and will provide income for the family in future years, or where it is clear at an early stage in the proceedings that the party concerned will be able to meet any reasonable order (*B* v *B* (1990) 20 Fam Law 335). Be very careful, if you decide that a professional valuation is necessary, that it focuses on relevant issues including the value of the business as security to raise funds and any financial benefits or benefits in kind which accrue to the shareholder.

Similar difficulties arise in respect of farms which are generally to be regarded as asset rich and cash poor. The major family asset is almost certainly unrealisable, often tied up in larger family arrangements, and the former wife's entitlement on divorce will reflect this. In such a case it can be very helpful if acting for a wife to instruct experienced accountants and land agents. There may be land or property that can be sold or transferred, and there will almost certainly be financial benefits to the family from the business arrangements which will need to be quantified.

An award must not be made which damages the business to a degree which impairs its effectiveness.

The court will view realisable assets (such as stock exchange investments) in a different way from business assets when considering the division of family assets. Except in those rare cases where realisable assets are supporting a business the court will invariably treat realisable assets as being available either for transfer to the other clients, or as available to be realised to provide a lump sum or pay for legal costs. For practical considerations when seeking a valuation, *see* Chapter 3, para **3.8.1**.

8.1.9 *Duxbury* calculations

This is a method of calculating a lump sum award named after the case in which the formula was first used (*Duxbury* v *Duxbury* [1987] 1 FLR 7). The formula is intended to calculate a lump sum sufficient to provide (usually) the wife with a capital sum to generate income for her for the rest of her life on the basis that the capital sum will itself be used up in the process. The calculation takes into account age, life expectancy, future rates of inflation and income tax, rates of capital growth and income return. It can be helpful in appropriate cases but is only one factor to be considered. Simple calculations are to be found in the FLBA publication *At A Glance*. More complex cases may require the assistance of an accountant.

8.2 'Clean break' settlements

8.2.1 When appropriate

A 'clean break' settlement may be attractive to the client who wants to settle existing problems and put the past behind him. It is unlikely to be appropriate in a case where there is real uncertainty as to whether a client can provide for himself or herself without undue hardship, particularly where there are young children.

The length of the marriage will clearly be a significant factor. Where there has been a short marriage with no children it is likely that the court would order that there should be no provision or a modest lump sum payment to provide, for example, for a deposit on a property or retraining. The position is very different when there is a short marriage with a child and such cases always appear to be particularly hard on the former husband. In the case of a longer marriage there will be greater emphasis on the needs of the parties and in particular on post-retirement needs.

Be cautious of the client who insists at the start of the case that he wants a clean break and try to prevent him making hasty decisions; the choice will affect him for life.

8.2.2 Effect of recent legislation

Various pieces of recent legislation have had a major impact on the whole concept of a clean break in cases where there are children. Social Security Act 1986, s 24A and Social Security Act 1990, s 8 now permit the DSS to seek a court order for the repayment of benefits paid through income support to a parent caring for a liable parent's children. Similarly, whereas in the past an absent parent might have agreed to surrender his (it is usually the husband's) share in the equity of the matrimonial home on the basis that the children would receive no more than nominal maintenance, now the Child Support

Act 1991 applies irrespective of any such overall planning of the order. Make sure that when advising an absent parent you calculate his assessable income so that you can advise him as to what part of the child maintenance requirement he is likely to have to meet. His own housing requirements will form part of his exempt income and to that extent at least will be taken into account.

A possible way round this difficulty in future cases is to include a 'charge back' clause in the order providing that when the house is transferred to the wife it is transferred subject to a charge which becomes effective to the extent of any demand made on the husband in respect of maintenance. Such a clause has yet to be tested in the courts.

8.3 Lump sum orders

8.3.1 Lump sum payable by instalments

Remember that such an order can be varied as to time of payment. However, where payment of a lump sum or any part of it is deferred or payable by instalments, the court may order interest to be paid at a rate specified in the order from a specified date not earlier than the date of the order.

8.3.2 Lump sum payments as a fixed amount or as a percentage of net sale proceeds

When a lump sum payment is dependent on the sale of property, usually the former matrimonial home, a lump sum order expressed as a percentage of net sale proceeds is likely to be seen as fairer by both parties, particularly in the light of the current housing market. However, beware of the housing needs of a wife with children which may require a limit to be fixed.

8.4 Priority of claim after re-marriage

Where a party has re-married there are priorities in respect of the financial claims of his various dependants. The children of the first marriage have priority, followed by the children of the second marriage, then the first wife and finally the second wife.

8.5 Pensions

The client's loss of pension rights on divorce will be an important consideration in many cases. In those cases where the parties are nearing or have reached retirement age, the effect of the dissolution of the marriage can have potentially serious financial consequences for the former wife. There is concern that the real value of the loss of pension rights to one spouse, usually to the wife, as a result of divorce, is being ignored through inability accurately to value the loss and/or through lack of resources to compensate for loss.

It is essential that you should understand the different forms of pension provision and what value they may have. Detailed consideration is beyond the scope of this book, but the following points are important.

8.5.1 Forms of pension

Make sure that you are familiar with the different forms of pension provision—remember state pension, SERPS, company schemes, statutory schemes (public sector employees, civil service), private pension policies—and make sure you have appropriate disclosure.

8.5.2 Benefits

There may be:
(a) lump sum payable on retirement,
(b) pension entitlement on retirement,
(c) widow's pension payable following husband's death before or after retirement,
(d) lump sum payable to the husband's estate should he die in service, and
(e) life cover payable to the husband's estate in the event of his death.

8.5.3 Widow's pension

There are two classes of widow's pension: those where the surviving spouse will definitely get a pension on the death of a scheme member, and those where payment depends on the discretion of trustees.

8.5.4 Obtaining valuation of loss of present rights and future possible rights

In appropriate cases where the quantum merits the expense, you may need to use an actuary, but it is very important to explain exactly what you want from him (*see* Chapter 3, para **3.8.1**, and draft instruction letter to actuary and draft r.2.63 pensions questionnaire in Appendix 6). The FLBA *At a Glance* tables are useful as a general guide.

8.5.5 The private company scheme

The private company scheme of which the husband and wife are members may be valuable as a post-nuptial settlement (*B* v *B* (1993) *The Times*, 7 May 1993).

8.5.6 Compensating for loss of rights

Consider taking out appropriate insurance cover. This course can only be followed if the parties agree because the court has no power to order a party to take out a life policy. Alternatively, compensation may take the form of an increased lump sum payment immediately or by instalments to reflect the present value of future losses.

8.5.7 Judicial separation

In extreme circumstances consider whether judicial separation proceedings might be appropriate to preserve entitlement, but be extremely careful that preserving the marriage is enough to preserve the pension rights—in some instances cohabitation at the date of death or retirement is a pre-requisite for entitlement.

8.5.8 Provision for loss of pension rights and clean break

You must consider very carefully whether the wife will be in a position to support herself for the rest of her life. Be very careful about dismissal of Inheritance (Provision for Family and Dependants) Act 1975 claims—courts will probably not dismiss claims while there is a continuing periodical payments order and may require details of the position as it would be on the death of the husband (*Whiting* v *Whiting* [1988] 2 All ER 275).

Finally, remember that pension loss is only one factor to be taken into consideration when deciding the appropriate level of financial provision.

For a helpful, detailed consideration of this area refer to Robin Ellison's *Pensions in Divorce* (Pensions Management Institute 1991) and to David Salter's *Pension and Insurance on Family Breakdown* (Family Law 1993). The PMI has also published a useful report recommending rules of good practice in this area.

8.6 Child Support Act 1991

It is not within the remit of this book to consider the detailed provisions of the Child Support Act 1991 nor how the Act will work in practice. It is important to bear in mind, however, that it will have a profound effect on all cases involving children and a bearing on the manner in which the entire financial provision package is approached. The child maintenance requirement will have to be assessed prior to consideration of any capital settlement, and re-calculated in the light of any proposed capital adjustment. You will need to be able to make these calculations yourself, probably with the assistance of a computer programme package, both in order to advise your client and to assist the judge at any hearing. *See also* relevance to purported 'clean break' settlements in para **8.2** *above*.

8.7 Capital Gains Tax

8.7.1 General

A potential liability to CGT, whether it arises immediately or is deferred, needs to be borne in mind when considering the net asset position of the parties (re *Calderbank*) and the net result of all capital transfers between parties. Make sure that you are familiar with the elements of the tax and its workings and in particular with the exemptions and reliefs which may apply to avoid or reduce the liability in respect of disposals between spouses. O P Wylie's book *Taxation of Husband and Wife—The New Rules* (Butterworths 1991) is helpful.

As the end of the tax year approaches, review your files to see whether there should be any transfers of assets between spouses who have separated on an interim voluntary basis, in order that the transfers will count as between spouses. In these cases CGT will remain inherent and will not be payable until a subsequent disposal of the asset.

8.7.2 CGT and the former matrimonial home

In cases where an owner spouse has been absent from the matrimonial home for more than three years a proportion of the gain will be chargeable on the sale or transfer of the former matrimonial home. Where the property is transferred to the other spouse the client may, however, be able to invoke Extra Statutory Concession D6 (deeming continued occupation of the matrimonial home until the date of transfer, provided that he has not elected to treat any other property as his main residence). It will be a matter of calculating which is financially desirable, bearing in mind how much the property has increased in value during the three-year period and that financial resources may be fully stretched at the time of the divorce.

8.7.3 *Mesher* type orders (*Mesher* v *Mesher* [1980] 1 All ER 126)

This is where the matrimonial home is transferred into the joint names of the spouses and held on trust for sale until the youngest child reaches 18 or some other triggering event occurs. One spouse, normally the wife, and the children live there and the other party realises his share when the property is sold.

A charge to CGT is only likely to arise on a sale of the property, but you must be careful to explain this liability to the client who is not to remain in occupation of the property. If the order is treated by the Inland Revenue as creating a settlement (as appears to be current practice), then Capital Gains Tax Act 1979, s 104 will apply, giving exemption at the time of the triggering event and reducing the absent party's liability to any gain incurred between the triggering event and the actual sale.

8.7.4 Deferred charge orders

In this case, the property is held in the sole name of the occupying spouse and the other spouse is given a charge, commonly expressed as a percentage of net equity, over the property. The charge will be realisable on any agreed triggering event. The advantage of such an order is that any mortgage will also be transferred, thereby releasing the absent spouse from any mortgage repayment covenants and giving the occupying spouse the security of owning the house, albeit subject to the charge. The current Inland Revenue view is that a liability to CGT will arise on the enforcement of the charge (calculated by deduction of the repayment value of the charge at the date the order is made from the amount actually received when the charge is enforced). Note that a charge for a fixed sum should be exempt from CGT, but the benefits of a saving of CGT are likely to be outweighed by the advantage to the client of a fixed percentage charge.

8.8   Income tax

8.8.1   Personal allowances

You need to be familiar with the position in the first year of separation and thereafter and the effect of having a child or children living with your client permanently or for some part of the year, eg weekends, on his allowance entitlement. Remember that the additional allowance is available only once to each parent irrespective of however many children are living with him or her.

8.8.2   Mortgage interest relief

Between separation and divorce the person remaining in the property should pay the interest if this is feasible in order to qualify for interest relief. In the long term, however, the party remaining in occupation should enter into a legal obligation to pay the mortgage, which can be done with the assistance of maintenance payments from the other party. The party in occupation will then benefit from MIRAS and the other party will receive the limited amount of tax relief on the maintenance payments.

8.8.3   Taxation of maintenance payments

Detailed consideration of the current tax position relating to maintenance payments is beyond the scope of this work, but you should ensure that you are familiar with it. Make sure that as far as possible all payments made qualify for tax relief; they must be under written legal obligation or court order (if available) and made to a former spouse who has not re-married (including payments made to a spouse for the benefit of a child). If there is no maintenance for a separated spouse or if it is likely to be less than the difference between the married and single person's allowance it is usual to require maintenance for a child to be paid to the separated spouse in order to exploit the allowance in full for the benefit of the paying parent.

Child support assessments are dealt with in exactly the same way as new court orders.

Practitioners should also be familiar with the provisions for varying existing orders or agreements made before 15 March 1988 and for the tax treatment of such orders.

8.8.4   School fees orders

New school fees orders should not present a problem. They should be expressed as gross amounts and will normally have no tax consequences. The situation relating to orders originally made prior to 15 March 1988 is more complicated—O P Wylie's book referred to in para **8.7.1** *above* will help you.

8.8.5   Party living abroad or foreign national resident in this country

It will be necessary to keep tax considerations in mind continually in such a case, and particularly in relation to the effect of any order. For example, certain countries treat maintenance payments differently for income tax purposes. In some countries a capital sum is taxable (watch for this in those cases where maintenance can only be enforced as a capital sum). It is important that you take particular care to understand all the implications of the foreign tax position as well as the liability to tax here. The impact may be quite considerable, eg the US IRS taxes its nationals wherever they live on world wide income and capital transactions. Take expert advice.

8.9   Protecting property

8.9.1   Severing a joint tenancy

Where a property is held on a joint tenancy the question of whether to advise your client to sever the tenancy will depend on the circumstances of the case. It is an important consideration where your client or the other client is unwell and may die. There will always be an element of chance. It may be an appropriate step to advise your client to take where there are liabilities attaching to the property.

8.9.2 Class F charge

Where a Class F charge is registered against a property do not forget to extend the charge beyond decree absolute if appropriate.

8.10 Property abroad

8.10.1 English court orders in respect of property abroad

The English court can make an order relating to property abroad, but you must ensure, before seeking such an order, that it is enforceable in the country concerned. If an order is made you must be particularly vigilant regarding its formal implementation to ensure that any transfer is valid in that country.

Remember also that it is possible to obtain asset-freezing orders of limited duration in some countries.

8.10.2 Enforcement of an English order abroad

Enforcement abroad is fraught with difficulty and is likely to be expensive. Some jurisdictions insist on a re-hearing before enforcement. Even if the legal difficulties can be overcome there may be chauvinist attitudes to be challenged also, the strength of which should not be underestimated.

8.11 Welfare benefits

This is a major area of law in its own right and one with which the family practitioner needs to be familiar. While it is beyond the scope of this book to go into any detail there are two important considerations to bear in mind: make sure that your client is receiving all the benefit to which he/she is entitled, including, eg single parent premium, child benefit, and be careful to consider the impact of any settlement terms or court order on your client's benefit position, eg a lump sum which has the effect of removing your client from income support.

8.12 Enforcement

The most useful methods of enforcing a financial order are by judgement summons or oral examination. In the latter case, do not be afraid to conduct the examination yourself—you will be in the best position to ask relevant, searching questions. Remember also the provisions of the Maintenance Enforcement Act 1991.

8.13 Some matters to bear in mind when drafting a financial order

Increasingly, solicitors are drafting consent orders to reflect negotiated agreements. It is extremely important to get the order right, and there are many pitfalls. In particular it is essential to distinguish between what may be expressed in the body of the order and what should form part of the recital. There are now several useful reference works containing suitable precedents, eg SFLA *Precedents for Consent Orders* and Longman's *Matrimonial Precedents* which will assist you.

It is crucial to ensure that the order accurately reflects what is agreed and that nothing relevant is omitted. Pay particular attention to details which can easily be overlooked and which, even if not serious, can cause considerable annoyance to the client, eg maintenance payable in advance or arrears, duration of order in favour of a child not clearly expressed.

In a legal aid case, do not forget to account for the impact of the legal aid charge when drafting the order and make sure that provision is made for deferment of the charge.

Remember that undertakings can only be enforced in certain ways and are not on the whole as useful as orders. Try where possible to include the provision as an order.

Make sure that where claims are to be dismissed, all the relevant claims are dealt with, including claim for secured provision and Inheritance Act (Provision for Family and Dependants) Act 1975 claims where appropriate.

9 Specific Areas 3—Divorce and Emergency Proceedings

9 Specific Areas 3—Divorce and Emergency Proceedings

As with the previous specific area chapters it is the authors' intention to set out below some general considerations to be borne in mind and to provide a few pointers in areas of particular difficulty, rather than to provide a comprehensive guide to the law on the topics covered.

9.1 Divorce

9.1.1 General considerations

Remember that the divorce petition is essentially a means to an end. Provided that both parties agree that the marriage is at an end and provided that the matter is handled sensitively and in a conciliatory manner, there should rarely be an issue about this aspect of the proceedings. Difficulties may arise when one party does not accept that the marriage is at an end or where the filing of the petition is connected with a more short-term objective, usually emergency proceedings, when a petition may need to be filed quickly, and will frequently have to be based on the 'immediate' fact of unreasonable behaviour. A weak application for a domestic violence injunction, for example, will be strengthened by the existence of a divorce petition. In such circumstances it is important not to lose sight of the long term objective of achieving an undefended divorce and the usual care should be taken in the drafting to ensure that no further unnecessary distress is caused to the other party by the allegations made.

9.1.2 The undefended petition

If you know that the petition will not be defended, it is good practice to rely on the mildest evidence available, eg two-year separation and consent if that is an option. If it is necessary to rely on the fact of unreasonable behaviour, draft the allegations in as mild a form as possible, while ensuring that the petition still contains sufficient evidence of irretrievable breakdown to convince the court. Bear in mind that different courts tend to apply different standards. In appropriate cases it is helpful to send a copy of the petition to the other party for agreement before filing. Do ensure, however, that you have a clear timetable for agreement so that the petition does not sit around unfiled indefinitely.

If the proposed petition is on the fact of separation, consider whether it is preferable for your client to be the respondent, when an application can be made under MCA 1973, s 10 to delay decree absolute until financial matters have been dealt with.

9.1.3   Adultery

Remember that if adultery is not agreed it must be proved.

As it is no longer necessary to name the co-respondent, you should consider carefully with your client the likely reaction from the other party of doing so. Although your client may be anxious to name the co-respondent it may cause unnecessary aggravation to do so. There is unlikely to be any advantage in naming the co-respondent.

9.1.4   Unreasonable behaviour

If you need to file an unreasonable behaviour petition, be careful not to go into too much detail in the petition; it is often more appropriate to reserve your right to make further allegations, thereby indicating to the other party that there are further, possibly more serious allegations that might be made if it proves necessary to do so.

9.1.5   Statement of arrangements for children

FPR 1991, r 2.2, provides that the statement of arrangements in respect of the children should be 'if possible agreed with the respondent'. There is a danger in attempting to comply with this rule that the other party may take the opportunity to issue a petition first. The rule does not make prior agreement of the statement mandatory but it is clearly more conciliatory to try to do so, unless you have good reason to believe that the statement is unlikely to be agreed or that giving notice of your intention to issue proceedings may be detrimental to your client, eg in domestic violence proceedings.

The SFLA has recommended that good practice entails

'advising clients that on receipt for approval from the other spouse's solicitors of a statement and/or particulars of a petition, and other than in exceptional circumstances, clients should not file their own petition first without giving the other party at least five working days' written notice of their intention to do so.'

9.1.6 Defending a petition

It will be only in rare cases that you will find yourself advising a client to defend a petition. It is an expensive process and can only further aggravate the anger and distress of the parties while achieving little, if anything, worthwhile at the end of the day. However, you may find yourself representing a client who, at least initially, is unable to accept that the marriage is over. It is important to make the distinction between this case and that of the client who acknowledges that the marriage is over but disputes the allegations made in the petition.

When the client does not consider that the marriage has broken down, it may be appropriate to consider 'blocking' the divorce at least temporarily by filing an answer denying each of the allegations and that the marriage has broken down, while exploring the possibility of reconciliation. It may simply be a question of biding your time and going through the motions, in order to allow the client to come to terms with what is happening, in the hope that when he attends the pre-trial review you are able to stage a diplomatic retreat on appropriate terms.

When the breakdown of the marriage is not an issue and your client merely wishes to contest the particular allegations made, it should be possible to reach a compromise which will enable the decree to be obtained undefended. If there are harmful allegations relating to finance or to children it will be important to negotiate their removal from the petition before allowing it to proceed. One possibility is to agree to the petition proceeding on the basis that the other party has acknowledged that your client does not accept the allegations in the petition. In this way you are not bound by *res judicata* should the allegations be raised again in subsequent proceedings. This can be indicated in the acknowledgement of service.

If the other party insists on filing a lengthy and objectionable unreasonable behaviour petition, then it may be necessary to file a cross-petition in order to enable a 'watering down' of the petition to be negotiated.

9.1.7   Defended divorce and legal aid

Once an answer has been filed your client will be entitled to apply for legal aid to continue to prosecute the divorce. Unless the statutory charge applies as a costs deterrent there is a real danger, which you as the solicitor must seek to avoid, of ending up with a dispute of inappropriate proportions. It is becoming increasingly difficult to obtain legal aid for a defended divorce where a client accepts that the marriage has broken down and is merely contesting the allegations, unless there is good reason to defend, for example if an allegation is made which might be relevant in a subsequent ancillary relief application.

9.1.8   Alternatives to divorce

Judicial separation proceedings

Judicial separation is rare but may be appropriate if your client has a fundamental objection to divorce, usually on religious grounds. It can also be a useful alternative where there is a large widow's pension and the loss of pension rights on divorce cannot be compensated for in any other way—(*see* Chapter 8, para **8.5.7**).

The court is empowered in the proceedings to make all the orders in respect of financial provision and children that it could in divorce proceedings. Bear in mind, however, that the same orders, apart from capital provision, may also be obtained in other proceedings.

Do not encourage your client to use judicial separation proceedings as a tactic; for example, a client who accepts that the marriage is over but wants to make things as difficult as possible for the other party should be persuaded that it will not help in the long run. Remind him that the other party may in any event apply for a divorce after five years' separation.

Nullity

Decrees of nullity are extremely rare, but where such a decree is appropriate some clients find it important psychologically for the marriage to be dissolved as a nullity and not by means of divorce. Most frequently, those seeking a nullity are those who have married for immigration purposes. In those cases, remember that you need to ensure that the statutory grounds of nullity are met.

9.2 Emergency proceedings

9.2.1 General considerations

Any emergency will be extremely disruptive and you may have to resist the desire not to take it on! Not only will you have to lay aside all your other cases to deal with it, but you will also find that it can take a disproportionately heavy emotional toll. It is therefore very important not to take on too many such cases.

It is essential if you are to deal effectively with an emergency application, which can of course materialise suddenly in the middle of what has been a routine case, that you have a well organised office and the proper systems to ensure that your other cases do not suffer and that you are able to act swiftly and efficiently to deal with the crisis.

Some cases are so urgent that you will take the client to court without papers, dealing with the case on oral evidence only and giving undertakings to file documents, and you will need to make a careful judgement as to whether this is appropriate. It is more likely that you will have at least a limited time to prepare. You may be able to test the urgency by suggesting a later date for an application to your client and judging his reaction.

It is important not to lose sight in the heat of the moment of the question of costs. When acting for a private client make sure that you are in funds before you make the application; this is an expensive form of litigation. If your client is entitled to legal aid you must obtain an emergency certificate before applying to the court and you should ensure that the legal aid forms are signed at the earliest opportunity (*see* Chapter 10, para **10.5.5**).

It is important that every family law solicitor learns at an early stage how to deal with an emergency application and much the best way to do so is to have the opportunity to follow a case through with a more experienced colleague (charging the client for one solicitor).

For strategic considerations, *see* Chapter 3, para **3.2.5**. A useful reference work for such applications is Fricker—*Family Courts: Emergency Remedies and Procedures* (2nd edn) Jordan and Sons, 1992.

9.2.2 Domestic violence injunctions

Have all your forms on the word processor, so that they are readily available and you can concentrate on extracting the essential facts from the client. Do not be coy about asking very personal questions or recording abusive language. Have a camera available to photograph injuries; it is often easier than describing them. It is essential to have a comprehensive check list to remind you of the ground to be covered (*see* Appendix 8).

Make sure that the terms of any ouster injunction you apply for are specific, identifiable and practical enough given the layout of the property to be of any use to your client.

It may on occasion be necessary for you to make emergency accommodation arrangements for a client and children in which case you will need to have ready access to telephone numbers of local women's aid refuges.

9.2.3   Emergency financial applications; MCA 1973, s 37 *Anton Piller* orders, *Mareva* injunctions

When applying for a financial injunction, it is important that your client understands that he will have to give an undertaking to the court on the granting of the injunction to pay damages and that he understands the consequences of this. Make sure also that he understands that such an application is likely to be very expensive.

It is essential that the application is as specific as possible. Important guidelines as to the execution of *Anton Piller* injunctions are set out in *Universal Thermosensors* v *Hibben and others* [1992] 3 All ER 257.

9.2.4   Service

Make sure you have photographs of the person on whom the injunction is to be served. Use a reliable process server, and remember that the order is not enforceable until it is served. If there is a power of arrest, make sure that the order is served on the defendant before papers are served on the police.

Service must be personal, and a solicitor cannot accept service on his client's behalf. If, therefore, you wish to arrange to serve an injunction in a less aggressive manner than by process server, you should arrange with the other solicitor to serve the injunction on the other party at the solicitor's office.

In appropriate cases DSS offices are useful places to serve documents!

9.2.5 Committal

In the event that an order is breached which is enforceable by committal notice, particular care must be taken that every detail of the order, the committal notice and service is correct as the liberty of the subject is at stake.

9.2.6 Child abduction

It need hardly be said that it is extremely difficult, traumatic and expensive to recover a child who has been removed to another jurisdiction, even when the child has been removed to a Convention country, and that it is very important therefore to take all possible steps to prevent an abduction from occurring. This will require you to exercise your skill and common sense in assessing whether there is a real likelihood of abduction. There may be indicators such as relatives living abroad, property held abroad, links with airlines, or the child may have dual nationality.

It is also important to consider whether a client is exaggerating the probability of an abduction attempt, and to explain to the client that too much pressure on the Home Office system to prevent abductions will remove resources from genuine cases.

In some cases a party may surrender his passport into the custody of a solicitor. Be very careful in such a situation as a potential conflict of interest may arise and there may be considerable difficulties for the solicitor should an undertaking given be broken. For guidance in this matter *see* the article in the *Law Society's Gazette*, 1 July 1992. Further advice can be obtained from the Law Society's Legal Practice Directorate. In the case of a child with dual nationality it is possible at some foreign embassies to register a request that no passport be issued for that child.

Abduction cases happen infrequently but when they do speed of response will be critical. Be sure that there is someone in the office who has all the practical information required at his fingertips, including the telephone number of the Lord Chancellor's Department, consular and Central Agency numbers in relevant countries, and relevant agencies. 'REUNITE' (*see* Appendix 4) can provide extremely useful advice. Make sure that you have available clear descriptions and photographs of the children.

You will need to familiarise yourself with the distinctions between the terms of the Hague and the European Conventions. For example, a party wishing to recover a child under the terms of the European Convention must have a residence or custody order in his favour, whereas under the Hague Convention parental responsibility is sufficient.

If you are acting for a parent who removes a child in breach of an order and you are being asked to disclose the child's whereabouts, you must tell the client that if you are ordered by the court to disclose the whereabouts of the child you will do so.

The Lord Chancellor's Department has a panel of child abduction solicitors to whom parents of children abducted to this country may be referred for representation. Panel members are recruited periodically as the need arises.

10 Legal Aid

10.1 Forms of legal aid available
- 10.1.1 Green Form scheme (advice and assistance)
- 10.1.2 Legal aid in family proceedings
- 10.1.3 Legal aid certificates for non-matrimonial (civil) proceedings
- 10.1.4 Applications under Child Abduction and Custody Act 1985
- 10.1.5 ABWOR (assistance by way of representation)
- 10.1.6 When legal aid is not available

10.2 Explaining legal aid to the client
- 10.2.1 Advising as to eligibility
- 10.2.2 Explaining how the system works

10.3 Your duty to the client and to the Legal Aid Board
- 10.3.1 Effect of legal aid certificate on relationship with client
- 10.3.2 Duty to the Legal Aid Board

10.4 The statutory charge
- 10.4.1 The scope of the charge
- 10.4.2 Enforcement
- 10.4.3 Explaining to the client
- 10.4.4 Minimising the impact

10.5 Procedure
- 10.5.1 Green Form scheme
- 10.5.2 Certificates covering matrimonial proceedings
- 10.5.3 Children Act 1989 proceedings
- 10.5.4 Non-matrimonial (civil) proceedings
- 10.5.5 Emergency legal aid
- 10.5.6 ABWOR

10.6 Taxation
- 10.6.1 When to submit the bill
- 10.6.2 Remuneration rates
- 10.6.3 Taxation process

10.7 Obtaining payment from the Legal Aid Board
- 10.7.1 Green Form

10 Legal Aid

This chapter is intended as a basic guide to legal aid for those solicitors whose clients are for the most part privately funded or for those
joining a legal aid practice having trained elsewhere, rather than for
the legal aid practitioner who will be familiar with the procedural
and strategic aspects of legal aid. The fact that a party is legally
aided will have implications for the conduct of a case both in terms
of practical matters such as timing and in matters of strategy. It may
fall upon the solicitor in a private client practice to act from time to
time for a legally aided client and it is also important that the solicitor whose own client is not himself legally aided but whose client's
spouse is fully understands the procedures involved and the impact
of legal aid on the case and its final outcome, particularly as to costs
and the effect of the legal charge. You should refer to the Legal Aid
Handbook 1993.

10.1   Forms of legal aid available

The following types of legal aid are available for proceedings in the
jurisdiction to those resident in or out of the jurisdiction:

10.1.1   Green Form scheme (advice and assistance)

The purpose of the scheme is to permit a client to receive financial
assistance for legal advice prior to the issue of a legal aid certificate,
which can take several weeks to obtain. It covers advice and assistance, up to a specified amount equivalent to two hours of work (or
three if a petition is drafted), including correspondence, drafting
divorce petition, and completing a legal aid application. Cover is
immediate on signing the form. Extensions of the financial limit can
be applied for (*see* para **10.5.1**). The scheme is particularly helpful to
the solicitor who does not wish to take a litigious approach to family
law issues as it allows time for negotiation before proceedings are
issued. However it has recently been severely limited in terms of

eligibility. Only a client on income support or with a net disposable income of less than £61 per week is currently entitled to benefit from the scheme.

The hourly rate payable is prescribed annually and published each April in the *Law Society's Gazette*.

10.1.2   Legal aid in family proceedings

It is available for:

Matrimonial proceedings

Legal aid is available for representation on ancillary matters, such as an injunction or ancillary relief application, but not for the divorce itself (Green Form), unless the petition is defended (*see* Chapter 9, para **9.1.7**), to be heard in open court or where by reason of physical or mental incapacity it is impracticable for the party to proceed without representation. It includes all assistance usually given to a client by a solicitor, including preparation for and representation at court proceedings and also steps taken to achieve a negotiated settlement. The grant of legal aid is subject to means and merit testing.

Eligibility depends on financial circumstances and on the merits of the case. The financial assessment to determine eligibility is dealt with by the DSS in Preston. The client's contribution is now payable by monthly instalments during the lifetime of the case until the certificate is discharged. If at any stage in the case the contributions paid appear likely to exceed the total costs of the proceedings the solicitor may apply on Form CLA 34 for future payments to be waived (Civil Legal Aid Regulations 1989 (as amended), reg 52(2)). (*See* also para **10.8** *below*.)

The merits of the application are considered by the local area office.

Free-standing Children Act 1989 proceedings

These are divided into 'special' proceedings and other proceedings. Special Children Act proceedings are prescribed by Legal Aid Act 1988, s 15 (3C) and are proceedings for care and supervision orders, child assessment orders and emergency protection orders (including extension and discharge applications). Legal representation is available without means or merit testing to parents including unmarried fathers, children or those with parental responsibility. For the same proceedings, in the case of those who are required to be parties or are applying to be joined, the merits but not the means test will apply. Other proceedings under the Act are dealt with in the normal way, with means and merit testing.

An application under CA 1989 under, eg s 8, made in the context of divorce proceedings will not require a separate certificate but will be covered under the matrimonial certificate.

Injunctions under DVMPA 1976 (Domestic Violence and Matrimonial Proceedings Act 1976)

Applications outside divorce proceedings are covered—both means and merit tests apply.

Wardship

Clients involved in private wardship proceedings (wardship in the public law sphere having been effectively withdrawn following Children Act 1989) may apply—means and merit tests apply.

10.1.3 Legal aid certificates for non-matrimonial (civil) proceedings

Confusingly, the term 'civil legal aid certificates' is used to cover both matrimonial and non-matrimonial certificates in applications in the family law field. For example, you may need to apply for a civil legal aid certificate when the client is unmarried, has not recently cohabited and where there are no children so that the alternatives referred to above are not available, eg in the case of an application for an injunction within a claim for damages for assault.

10.1.4 Applications under Child Abduction and Custody Act 1985

A person who has applied under The Hague Convention or The European Convention through the Central Authority of England and Wales (Lord Chancellor's Department) and who has instructed a solicitor in England is eligible regardless of means and will not be required to make any contribution. This is not the case if the client is the respondent to the application.

10.1.5   ABWOR (assistance by way of representation)

This is less common but covers civil cases in the magistrates' courts, eg applications under Domestic Proceedings and Magistrates' Courts Act 1978 such as separation, maintenance and defended adoption. It also covers applications before Mental Health Tribunals. The financial eligibility requirements are equivalent to the old Green Form scheme scales. The Legal Aid Handbook describes ABWOR as 'a half-way house between advice and assistance and civil legal aid'.

10.1.6   When legal aid is not available

Legal aid is not available for representation before a Child Support Act 1991 tribunal or any welfare benefit tribunals.

10.2   Explaining legal aid to the client

10.2.1   Advising as to eligibility

It is very important to remember that you have a duty to advise your client of his entitlement to legal aid even if you do not deal with such cases yourself and to record such advice in writing. You should also bear in mind that if your client's circumstances change significantly for the worse during the course of the case, he may thereby become eligible for legal aid and must be advised accordingly. The reverse is of course also true.

The question of payment of costs should be raised with the client at the earliest suitable opportunity (*see* Chapter 2, para **2.3.9**). Depending on the type of legal aid sought, you will have to consider the merits of the case and whether the client will meet the financial qualifications, advising him also of the likely size of his contribution, which is always difficult. Current income and capital limits are published annually and listed in the April edition of the *Law Society's Gazette*.

10.2.2   Explaining how the system works

You must explain to the client that legal aid is by nature of a loan which has in many cases to be repaid by virtue of the statutory charge (*see below*, para **10.4**). The extent to which costs are incurred will have a direct bearing on what the client receives at the end of the case. You should also explain that even if the client is successful in obtaining orders for costs against the other party during the proceedings, such orders will not cover the entire legal aid bill and there may still be a liability to be met or protected by a charge at the end of the day.

An explanatory letter setting out this information in clear and simple language should be sent to the client following your first meeting. A precedent is included at Appendix 9.

It is also important that a similar explanation is given to a privately funded client in a case where the other party is legally aided. A further and important effect is that it will not in practical terms be realistic to expect to obtain an order for costs against a legally aided party. In the rare cases where the court considers an order to be appropriate it is usually expressed as 'not to be enforced without leave'. The application for leave to enforce can be made at any time and the court will conduct an enquiry into the party's means before an order is made. Make sure the client understands that there is a considerable volume of legal aid administration involved before, during and after the case which may mean, for instance, that he will not immediately receive any moneys due to him in the proceedings (*see also below*, para **10.4**).

Make sure, too, that a client who is paying a contribution under a legal aid certificate understands the importance of paying the contribution instalments promptly and the consequences of failing to do so, including the possible discharge of the certificate with very little warning. Remember this could happen at a crucial stage in the proceedings.

10.3 Your duty to the client and to the Legal Aid Board

10.3.1 Effect of legal aid certificate on relationship with client

The normal relationship between the solicitor and his client is expressly preserved by the Legal Aid Act 1988. Acting for a legally aided client should not affect the quality of the service you offer. There are, however, costs constraints which prevent the client from litigating indiscriminately and running up unnecessary costs; the fact that the Legal Aid Board (LAB) has to approve certain steps and particular expenditure if it is to be allowed on taxation can be a useful restraint for curbing excessive demands from your client. Remember that legal aid is not retrospective so that up to the date of issue of a legal aid certificate your relationship with your client is as a private client (unless on a Green Form).

10.3.2 Duty to the Legal Aid Board

The privileged nature of your relationship with the client will be affected when the wishes of the client conflict with the interests of the LAB. You are under a duty to inform the LAB of any abuse of legal aid. The abuse is likely to take such forms as a failure to disclose a relevant change in financial circumstances, or insistence on pursuing a case when it is unreasonable to do so.

You should inform the client that you are passing this information to the LAB and warn him of the possible consequences, including the discharge of the certificate or even its revocation, in which case the LAB will have the power to recover from the client the entire costs incurred under the certificate.

Remember that if there is a change in your client's circumstances his or her entitlement to legal aid may be affected; maintenance payments to a wife and/or children, even if voluntary, may take the wife outside the legal aid limits or affect her contribution. It may be necessary to apply for reassessment.

If you believe that the other party is using legal aid inappropriately it is now possible to notify the LAB, who will investigate.

10.4 The statutory charge

10.4.1 The scope of the charge

The legal aid fund has a first charge on any property recovered or preserved by the assisted person in the proceedings to the extent that payment is not recovered by the assisted person's contribution or in costs payable by the other party. The first £2,500 of money or value in property is exempt from the charge, as are periodical payments.

Be careful not to be party to any deliberate attempt to avoid the statutory charge. You have a duty to the legal aid fund not to manipulate the terms of a settlement in order to avoid the effects of the charge. Where for example the agreement provides for periodical payments only to a wife and a substantial lump sum payment to a child, the child's lump sum may be attachable if the LAB suspects that the form of the agreement is an attempt to avoid liability.

10.4.2 Enforcement

As the party's solicitor you are under a duty to report the receipt of any lump sum payment or the recovery or preservation of any property to the LAB. In the former case, you must pass on any cash you receive on behalf of the client, apart from the exempted sums referred to above, to the LAB. In the latter case the LAB may register a charge against the property.

Under Civil Legal Aid (General) Regulations 1989 (SI No 339), regs 96 and 97 enforcement of the statutory charge may be deferred, on payment of interest, provided that the money or property recovered or retained is to be used as a home for the party and/or the children and the order so specifies. The wording must be precise (*see* the SFLA publication *Precedents for Consent Orders*). The interest rate is high, and the interest can be rolled up if the assisted person wishes. Your client may wish to consider the possibility of repaying the moneys due to the Legal Aid Fund by increasing the mortgage rather than deferring the charge at interest.

10.4.3 Explaining to the client

It is vital that you explain the impact of the statutory charge on any financial settlement and that you ensure that the client has understood. Your initial explanatory letter to the client should cover this, but it will be worth repeating at later stages in the proceedings, particularly if any unusually expensive step is contemplated. You are required to provide the client with a copy of the Law Society's explanatory leaflet *The Statutory Charge*.

Remember to explain the effect of the charge to the client who is not legally aided but whose spouse is. It is all too easy to forget that the assisted person's costs will have to be met out of the family's funds at the end of the day.

10.4.4 Minimising the impact

Obtain orders for costs where you can.

Consider carefully what is in issue and avoid bringing property into dispute unnecessarily. For example, if the matrimonial home is in joint names, and the husband concedes that the wife's interest is not in dispute and the issue is restricted to what part of the husband's interest is to be transferred to the wife, then the statutory charge can only attach to that part of the husband's share which the wife recovers.

Because of the unified nature of family proceedings certificates a wide variety of issues can now be covered under one certificate and *all* these costs will be covered by the statutory charge if it applies. A dispute over residence of a child (perhaps following injunctive proceedings), followed by an ancillary relief application can mount up to a very large bill. Consideration should therefore be given as to whether particular steps are in fact necessary at any particular time, bearing in mind their potential impact on the charge.

The ramifications of the statutory charge are complex and there is not space here to consider the matter in great detail. It is, however, a most important issue that needs to be carefully studied in order to ensure that its impact on the particular case is understood by everyone involved, and its effect minimised where possible.

10.5 Procedure

10.5.1 Green Form scheme

Initial application

The client signs a Green Form (GF1) and using the key card produced by the LAB each April the solicitor calculates the client's disposable income and capital. Be careful to have an accurate system to record time used so that you know when you are reaching the limit and can if necessary apply in good time for an extension. Remember that disbursements count towards money allowed, but not VAT.

Extensions

Authorisation for an extension must be obtained before additional expenditure is incurred by making an application on Form GF3. Further extensions can be obtained as required.

Authorities

For certain steps prior authority is needed, eg to change solicitors, to advise a person resident outside England and Wales or to advise a child. Such applications should be made on Form GF5.

Schemes to replace contributory system

Prior to 5 April 1993 there was a contributory system for those with a disposable income up to a certain limit, which has now been significantly curtailed. A large number of prospective clients are no longer eligible and you and your firm should consider how you will deal with this situation. Some firms now operate their own schemes to assist those who would previously have received advice under the scheme on a contributory basis, in particular to enable them to have access to full legal aid, as the preparation of the application would normally have been dealt with under the Green Form scheme.

10.5.2 Certificates covering matrimonial proceedings

Applying for a certificate

Apply by post (blue CLA 2A and appropriate financial form (CLA 4A, or CLA 4B if claiming income support) and Form L17 completed by employer) to the local legal aid area office. The solicitor or guardian may apply on behalf of a child (Form CLA 4F). For a client resident outside the UK use Form CLA 4C.

You may, depending on your client's emotional state, complete the form straightaway at the first interview or give it to him to fill in at home, including Form L17.

The applicant must have reasonable grounds for taking the proceedings. Set out the application carefully in legible handwriting, dealing with the issues as legal problems. Careful drafting may avoid unhelpful limitations (*see below*). It can save time to attach a copy attendance note of your meeting with the client providing it sets out clearly your client's case and what is required. If you are not certain that your client's case merits legal aid, it may be appropriate to apply initially for a limited certificate, eg up to discovery only, in order to avoid the application being turned down.

As a general rule be careful when sending forms to the LAB that you do not obscure their colour, as this will delay their processing.

Rather than attaching a covering letter, use a compliments slip attached at the bottom of the form.

Once the application is lodged, the LAB will check the financial details with the DSS and in appropriate cases there will be a means assessment at the legal aid assessment office in Preston. It is important to warn your client to deal promptly with any communication he receives from Preston as any delay will hold up the issue of the certificate.

The length of time taken to process the application will vary regionally, but in London for example, it currently takes three to four weeks. The area office will not usually take calls except for emergency applications; all other enquiries must be dealt with by post. Remember that the certificate cannot be backdated.

Where there are different sets of proceedings

One certificate will now cover all proceedings which are family proceedings (as defined by MFPA 1984, s 32) and should be amended as the need arises. The client should be warned that any costs incurred under the certificate will fall under the statutory charge if the statutory charge applies, even if they do not relate to the proceedings in which the property to be charged is retained (*see above,* para **10.4.4**).

Amendments are applied for on Form CLA 30. Where a case is transferred to a higher court during the course of proceedings there is no need to amend the certificate.

Notification

When the certificate is issued, check the wording carefully. Any errors should be dealt with immediately. It is particularly important, if the certificate was initially granted by telephone, to check the date.

Once the certificate has been issued you should send a notice of issue and the top copy of the certificate to the court. You should also serve the notice on all other parties. Any subsequent amendments must be treated similarly. Do it straightaway before you forget. It is useful to keep all legal aid documents together on your file so that the history of legal aid is always to hand.

Limitations on certificate.

The certificate may be limited, eg requiring proceedings to be commenced in the family proceedings court, limited as to costs or in proceedings for defended divorce, up to the directions appointment only in the first instance.

If you consider the limitation to be inappropriate, raise the issue with the legal aid office immediately. As a general rule, for example, cases should not be started in the family proceedings court when they involve an international element, where a penal notice may be required, or where there are many parties involved.

Scope of certificate—instructing experts and counsel

Prior approval should be obtained from the LAB when certain steps are to be undertaken or disbursements incurred, eg an expert's report or DNA testing, to ensure that these costs will be allowed on taxation. Authorities are not retrospective. Apply on Form CLA 31. Even when authority is forthcoming you should obtain your client's consent before incurring any unusual expense, and explain to him that he may eventually be paying for it as part of his contribution or by virtue of the statutory charge. It is useful to have a standard letter to deal with this.

If specific authority is not requested or is not forthcoming the solicitor bears the risk that if the disbursement is not allowed on taxation, the solicitor may be personally liable if the client, despite agreeing to pay the disbursement himself, is not in a financial position to do so. An assistant solicitor should seek a partner's authority before incurring such a disbursement.

It may take some time for an application for authority to incur such expenses to be processed and this may have a bearing on whether you do make such an application. For example, if time is short and you would be seeking authority for an expert to report in a child-related case for which you have already obtained the leave of the court, you may consider proceeding in any event as the reasonable costs of such an expert are likely to be justifiable on taxation. Remember, however, that in such a case the LAB will only give authority if leave has already been obtained.

You do not require authority to instruct counsel in the higher courts, but you must inform counsel that it is a legal aid matter. You must, however, obtain authority before briefing leading counsel or two counsel. Authority to brief leading counsel does not include consultations unless specifically stated. Junior counsel may be asked to give an opinion as to why a leader is necessary. The instruction of leading counsel by the other party is a persuasive argument. If you wish junior counsel to be briefed as well as leading counsel you must ask specifically for this. The use of counsel will not be covered in the family proceedings court unless specifically authorised by the court. If, however, counsel is instructed the LAB will assess the total costs of the case and divide them between solicitor and counsel (the maximum fee principle).

If an application is turned down

There is a right of appeal to the area committee on a merits argument. Write a full letter of appeal and tell your client to go along in person to the appeal. Legal aid is not available to represent the client at the appeal. It may take some time for the appeal to be heard and in the meantime you are not covered for any work on that client's behalf.

10.5.3 Children Act 1989 proceedings

Applications for orders

For applications for s 8 orders and other orders under the Children Act *not* specifically covered by the special arrangements *(see below)* use form CLA 5 together with the appropriate financial forms *(see above,* para **10.5.2**).

Special Children Act proceedings (see above, *para **10.1.2**)*

The solicitor alone signs the application (Form CLA 5A). Provided that the completed form reaches the LAB within three working days of signature, the certificate is deemed to have been granted on the date the form is signed. This applies to parents, children (with or without guardian ad litem) and those with parental responsibility.

10.5.4 Non-matrimonial (civil) proceedings

The procedure will be as for a matrimonial proceedings certificate, but the forms will be different. Use form CLA 1 to apply together with the relevant forms (CLA 4A/B/F—*see above*, para **10.5.2**).

10.5.5 Emergency legal aid

In cases of urgency it may be appropriate to apply for emergency legal aid. The application enables the client to obtain legal aid quickly without full investigation of his means or the merits of his case. Application may be made by post (Form CLA 3 and other main forms as appropriate) when it will be dealt with within two to three days, or in cases of extreme urgency by telephone, with the relevant forms completed and despatched after legal aid has been granted. Make sure to note the reference number of the person who has granted the emergency certificate and to send in the forms within five working days. This facility must only be used where there is a genuine emergency.

You cannot fax an application to the LAB, but you may receive the result by fax from the LAB.

If the emergency certificate bears the same date as your Green Form scheme application, you should not claim under the Green Form, except where appropriate, for pursuing divorce proceedings for example. The aid is granted for a limited purpose and may be revoked if it transpires that the applicant is ineligible. Make sure the client understands this at the outset.

10.5.6 ABWOR

Application is made on Form ABWOR 1. Applications for prior authority or amendments to the certificate should be made on ABWOR 6 (ABWOR approval).

10.6 Taxation

10.6.1 When to submit the bill

The bill should not be submitted until the case is properly over (*see below*, para **10.6.3**). This includes implementation of the order (but not an application to enforce for which amendment is necessary) and will in some cases require careful judgement, for example if there are continuing problems with the implementation of a contact order. It may be necessary to amend the certificate to undertake continuing work, ie with a view to further applications.

10.6.2   Remuneration rates

Do not forget that there are now prescribed rates of remuneration for most family proceedings. Be careful to use the correct one for the proceedings for which you are claiming.

10.6.3   Taxation process

In common with other cases the authority to tax arises from either the court order or the discharge of the legal aid certificate. Bills are taxed in the appropriate court or courts if there have been proceedings in different courts. When instructing your costs draftsman ensure that you allow for correspondence with the LAB following the bill—otherwise there will be six or seven letters for which you will not be paid.

The bill must generally be lodged within three months of the order (or later with leave if there are problems with implementation). If there is no one with a financial interest in the bill (ie there is no *inter partes* element and the statutory charge will not apply), there will be a provisional taxation by a taxing officer (bills up to £15,000) or a district judge. Some courts require you to lodge the bill alone first with the bundle of papers thereafter, or the bill and the bundle immediately.

If there are parties who may have a financial interest in the bill (this may include your client if the statutory charge applies), you are obliged to send a copy of the bill to them explaining their right to be heard on taxation. Make it clear to your client that you are allowed to charge the legal aid fund for attending a taxation appointment (ie it may increase the amount of costs caught by the charge). When you lodge your bill with the court you must also certify that you have served all parties with copies of the bill as outlined above (Civil Legal Aid (General) Regulations 1989, reg 105A). A period of 21 days is allowed for representations to be made and if such representations are received a taxation appointment is fixed.

If provisionally taxed the bill will be returned with proposed reductions which you may either accept, or if you wish to be heard you may apply for a taxation appointment.

If counsel's fees have been reduced, you must check with his clerk whether the reduction is acceptable. If not, you must apply for a taxation appointment at which you represent counsel.

If you do not wish to apply for a taxation appointment, you should complete the bill, certify that the costings are correct, and certify that you consent on your own and your client's behalf to the signing forthwith of the taxing officer's certificate (otherwise he must wait 21 days). You must also certify that you have informed counsel of any reduction in his fees. It is useful to have a stamp with this endorsement which is then simply signed. The court will then send you an *allocatur* which forms the basis of your claim for costs from the LAB.

10.7 Obtaining payment from the Legal Aid Board

10.7.1 Green Form

Complete the back of the Green Form signed by the client and submit with covering form GF2 in duplicate to the area office. Costs are claimed on the basis of prescribed rates. If work spans more than one year (April to April) you must specify when the work was done and apply the appropriate rates.

The bill is subject to approval and if found reasonable will be paid. (If moneys are recovered from the other party in a case where no legal aid certificate has been issued, the statutory charge still operates but in this case in favour of the solicitor who may take Green Form costs from the sum recovered.) Do not forget that you must formally account to the client with a bill calculated on Green Form rates.

10.7.2 ABWOR

Complete form ABWOR 3 using prescribed rates. The same considerations apply as stated above for work spanning more than one year.

10.7.3 Bills assessed by the LAB

The LAB will assess any bills in cases in the family proceedings court and in any other cases where the total costs, including disbursements and counsel's fees (but not VAT), amount to £1,000 or less. Use Form CLA 17 with CLA 16 (*see below*). A bill submitted to the LAB will either be paid as asked or provisionally assessed and you will be given 21 days to object to any proposed reductions. You are responsible for notifying counsel of any proposed reduction in his fee and he is responsible for dealing directly with the LAB.

10.7.4   Claim following taxation

When claiming under a legal aid certificate following taxation, the claim is made on Form CLA 16. Make sure that you have the right certificate number on the form. Set out profit costs plus VAT as stated on the *allocatur*. The costs of the case and the costs of taxation are shown separately on the *allocatur* and care should be taken to include both elements. Include also disbursements plus VAT, and counsel's fees including VAT. If more than two counsel are involved, use extra forms.

Send the original *allocatur*, a copy of the taxed bill, and counsel's fee notes and Form CLA 16 in duplicate to the LAB who will pay you in due course. If you have not yet claimed under the Green Form scheme, you should do so at the same time.

10.7.5   *Inter partes* element

If the bill contains an *inter partes* element you must be careful to claim the entire amount of the bill, ie both legal aid and *inter partes* on Form CLA 16. The LAB will then negotiate with you as to how the contribution to be paid by the other party is to be collected. Your existing legal aid certificate will cover the costs of recovery of the amount due from the other party by way of costs, but remember that these costs may be caught in the statutory charge. If proceedings are necessary, you will be authorised to recover on the LAB's behalf, but make sure that you have your client's consent because of the statutory charge implications. Where costs/damages have been awarded but not recovered in full you are now required to complete a form 'Costs 1' which will ask for details of the debtor's employment, etc.

10.7.6   Payments by the LAB on account

You can apply for payments on account of disbursements of over £35, eg medical reports, valuations, as and when they arise. It is courteous in any event to explain in your letter of instruction to any expert that your client is legally aided and that there may be a delay in payment. Apply on Form CLA 28.

As a general rule you cannot apply for money on account of profit costs. This includes costs of solicitor agents. However, on the anniversary of the issue of the certificate you will receive from the LAB a Form CC1 requiring you to supply details of profit costs including VAT, disbursements to date, and what stage has been reached in the proceedings. You are then entitled to claim a percentage of your costs on account. The form must be completed and returned within the time limit specified on the form. The other exception to this rule is if your firm is suffering financial hardship (*see* Chapter 11, para **11.2.2**).

10.8 Discharging the certificate

The certificate may be discharged on payment of the final bill unless you have indicated that there is further work to be done or there are costs to be recovered. Alternatively you can apply for discharge but you will need your client's consent to do this. If this is not forthcoming the Law Society may send a 'show cause' letter, asking the client to show cause why the certificate should not be discharged. This procedure applies to cases where the client is acting unreasonably or failing to give instructions, etc, as well as on more straightforward occasions. If it is not answered then the certificate will be discharged. If you do not discharge the certificate you may find yourself inundated with irrelevant computer generated correspondence from the LAB for years to come!

As mentioned *above*, the client's contribution (if any) remains payable until the certificate is discharged so that it is particularly important to arrange for discharge as soon as possible after the case is over. Beware, however, that you must ensure full implementation of any order that has been made; otherwise you will not be covered for additional work which may be necessary, particularly following the recent cuts under the Green Form Scheme.

11 The Office

11   The Office

Now that we have looked at the issues of client care, personal development, techniques and strategy of running a case, it is the turn of the office itself to come under more detailed scrutiny. Careful attention to the organisation and management of the office is as important as the legal and personal side of the work. Although family law experts are to be found in a wide variety of offices ranging from the small legal aid practice to a department within a large city firm, many of the same issues, such as quality of work, efficiency of staff and systems, costs structure and billing, profitability and forward planning must be confronted and will be similar in all but scale.

The chapter is divided into two sections, the first concerned with the process of setting up a new family law practice (specifically a legal aid practice, but much would apply also to a private client practice), and the second with the development of an existing practice, including how to justify the existence of a family law department within a wider practice. Both sections deal with the vital matter of developing and maintaining a client base. For the legal aid practice the question of whether to apply for a legal aid franchise will also have to be tackled.

There is inevitably overlap between the two sections and indeed with the earlier chapters dealing with the solicitor and his team and with client care (Chapters 1 and 2) as these are both essential features of a successful practice.

SETTING UP A SMALL LEGAL AID PRACTICE

11.1 Planning

11.1.1   Research

Before you decide to set up in business on your own or in partnership with others, make that you understand fully what you are letting yourself in for! It will require extremely hard work particularly in the first few years as your client base begins to build up, and there can be a large financial risk, particularly if you have to mortgage your home to raise capital. In the early days you will need to be financially very cautious and be prepared to pay yourself the minimum salary possible. On the other hand, you will be your own master and able to develop the style and tone of practice that you want, which will be immensely rewarding.

Thorough research is essential. This will involve ascertaining the market for the services you intend to provide in the particular location you have in mind. These days it is also important to consider what range of services you wish to provide—the 'general practice' which knows a little about everything is becoming a thing of the past. Some related areas of work demand a level of expertise which will only be justified economically by a large case load, eg immigration. It is very helpful to talk to others who have recently established similar firms and to learn from their mistakes as well as their successes.

If you are setting up the firm jointly with others, make sure that you share a common view of the type of firm you wish to have and a common approach to working practices. It is important, too, that you consider such issues as, for instance, the possibility of one of the partners becoming seriously ill or unavailable for an extended period in the near future, and whether the others are willing to make arrangements to deal with the inevitable disruption. This can be particularly difficult in the early years of the business.

11.1.2 Business plan

Your initial business plan will be an important document and essential to persuade a bank of the viability of your proposals. This will contain projections of income and expenditure and a marketing plan. Be realistic. Calculate the projection of income on a low but realistic 'cost per case' basis with again a low but realistic estimate of your caseload and its rate of growth. Remember how long it takes for cases to come to a close and be realistic about time to obtain payment (whether private or legal aid cases). If you will be holding significant sums in a client account, calculate the likely income from interest on those sums after meeting interest due to clients.

In relation to expenditure, include everything. Obvious items are rent due, salaries, insurance, etc, but do not forget the paper clips and rubber bands! It is those sorts of items which, if not carefully monitored, can easily get out of hand and upset the original projections.

If you are going to be computerised, a spreadsheet programme from the outset will probably prove invaluable. If not, prepare a manual cash flow projection for the next 12 months. Manoeuvre payments that are flexible to avoid 'heavy payment' months in those items such as rent, indemnity insurance and VAT payments.

In terms of a marketing plan, think carefully about how you wish to project yourself. If aiming at a local clientèle, use the local paper, otherwise a brochure sent to professional colleagues, such as accountants, surveyors or non-family law firms. Think about sponsoring events which will attract clients, a local sports team, a seat in a beleaguered theatre, or an art gallery for instance.

In setting up any new practice, but particularly a legal aid practice, you must make sure that you have sufficient capital. Cash flow is always a serious problem, however promptly you submit bills to the Legal Aid Board. It is advisable to ensure that you begin with sufficient funds (probably borrowed) to keep the business running for at least six months on the basis that there is likely to be very little income during that time.

11.1.3　Partnership deed

You will also wish to draw up a partnership deed covering such matters as capital, drawings, maternity allowance, holiday entitlement. If you have or plan to have salaried partners, they will need to be given appropriate indemnities. If, rather than setting up your own practice, you are considering joining an existing firm as a salaried partner, look for an indemnity clause (remembering that the indemnity is only as good as the people behind it) and look carefully at any restrictive covenants which may be excessively onerous.

It is important to make proper provision for holidays for yourself and other partners as well as for your staff, but ensure that partners stagger their holidays.

11.2　Arranging finance

11.2.1　Dealing with the bank

Remember that all aspects of financial arrangements with a bank are negotiable. In particular you can negotiate interest rates, charges and commission. Be alert to the 'arrangement fee' which may not be mentioned but is usually one per cent. You may find the manager simply stating that the charge will be 'x', but push a little and you may find it turns into 'y'. Solicitors are attractive clients for a bank. Bank lending rates are usually expressed as a percentage over base rate and a new business can expect to pay three to four per cent above base rates to begin with. As you become established this can be re-negotiated from time to time. Try to secure your loan against assets of the business, eg freehold premises, rather than against private assets such as your own home. If you have to charge your own home try to ensure that the charge is redeemed at the earliest opportunity.

11.2.2 Legal Aid Board payments

Arrange as soon as possible to receive payment on a fortnightly, rather than monthly, basis, and remember that the Legal Aid Board can make 'one off' payments where you can show that there are outstanding bills awaiting payment and you will suffer financial hardship if an earlier payment is not made. You need to be in a position to quote certificate numbers and amounts of the bills rendered, so careful records should always be maintained (*see below*, para **11.3.4**). For details of how to apply see *The Legal Aid Handbook 1993*.

Always apply for disbursements on account as they arise and pay disbursements as soon as funds are received, otherwise you may end up with distorted cash balances, leading you to believe you are in a better financial position than you are.

11.3 Setting up the office

11.3.1 Selecting premises

Consider your intended clientèle and aim the office at their requirements. For a legal aid practice you will need to be locally based and visible, probably in a high street, on a site with easy access by public transport. Being near to a court which deals with family law matters is also helpful. Work out whether there are any local firms near you who will either compete with or complement your service. At least one local firm nearby is valuable, if only to swear affidavits and borrow envelopes from etc, if in a crisis and the stationer has let you down. Think how the area you have selected will develop and whether you will need to move to larger premises if you expand. Do not take on too long a lease which may then be difficult to dispose of. Freeholds are attractive as assets but tie up capital and may be hard to sell.

11.3.2 Employing staff

In the initial stages, employ as few staff as you can. A secretary can also double as a receptionist. Increase the numbers slowly as business develops. However, it is worth always having a professional bookkeeper from the outset because it is not cost effective to deal with the firm's bookkeeping yourself and it is often an area in which new firms experience problems.

11.3.3 Setting up systems

Be sure to start with systems that will grow with your practice and do not underestimate what you are likely to need in the foreseeable future, eg the number of telephone lines. While you may start with a manual accounting system you should budget to move on to a computerised system as early as possible.

Look always at methods of spreading payment for large items of office equipment, eg leasing, paying by instalments, deferred payment, but be aware that these will have financing costs and it will be a matter of judgement as to which method of payment you choose. Be wary of leasing equipment over too long a period as it may become obsolete. Again, all leasing arrangements are negotiable and you need to be ruthless, pitching one company against another to ensure that you get the best deal for your requirements. Make sure, too, that in order to avoid expensive mistakes you take very careful advice before embarking on the leasing or purchase of any equipment. A cash flow projection is essential.

11.3.4 Accounting—some basic points to remember

Where work is to be paid for by the LAB, be sure to keep a running record of when bills are submitted, the profit cost element of each bill, and how much the LAB owes you at any one time.

Do not process legal aid bills as invoices until they are paid, or you will end up with an earlier VAT liability. It is also advisable to keep a running record of VAT liability.

When you receive money on account from a non-legally aided client, make sure that you submit an interim bill as soon as possible.

11.3.5   Using management information

Like running any small business, using management information is crucial. Be aware of the profit costs billed by each fee earner and whether the total for the firm or department is meeting the monthly expenditure. Keep these records as it is useful to compare results year on year. A firm or department target should be identified. Personal targets are more difficult and if not handled by managers sensitively can be demoralising for junior staff. Work in progress needs most careful monitoring to ensure that it is realistic and regular housekeeping is essential.

11.4   Developing a client base

11.4.1   Having a welcoming office

The importance of first impressions has already been mentioned in Chapter 2. If your firm is a local firm relying on clients who will walk in off the street it is essential that you have welcoming premises and reception staff so that new clients are not intimidated by their first contact with the firm. Most legal aid practices favour shop front offices which permit the prospective client to inspect the premises before entering. It is important to create a welcoming and sympathetic impression while at the same time being, and being seen to be, efficient and business-like. While you will need to provide private waiting areas for some clients, eg the battered wife, it is reassuring for the future client to be able to see other ordinary-looking people with children and shopping in the office. Thought should be given to the layout of the premises as a whole and to the needs of the client. It is useful to have access for the disabled. It may be appropriate to have some toys in the reception area or in the solicitor's office. Make sure there are lavatories available for the use of clients.

Be careful to ensure client confidentiality so that clients' files are not left where they may be seen by other clients (eg in the reception area if the receptionist is also a secretary). The reception area should always be tidy and clean and look well organised.

The importance of your own presentation and demeanour is dealt with in Chapter 1, para **1.5**.

11.4.2   Advertising

Advertising locally is extremely helpful when setting up a new practice dependant on local clients. Consider advertising in Yellow Pages, local newspapers and radio, and indirectly by writing articles or giving interviews for the local media. Focused advertising can be useful if you have a specialism, eg injunctions. In the interests of saving costs, consider not employing graphic designers for such matters but instead producing the documents yourself. Look at advertisements that you yourself respond to and incorporate ideas into your own style.

11.4.3   Establishing and maintaining a high professional profile

It is also essential to make yourself known to local professionals in the hope that they will then refer work to you. Offer to give talks to local groups, eg a police domestic violence unit, child protection team, magistrates, local Citizen Advice Bureaux. Attend all local court meetings, join appropriate committees. Join the duty solicitor scheme. Do your own advocacy as far as possible, so that your face is familiar in the courts. When at court, talk to the staff and explain your new firm to them. A surprising number of clients are referred to solicitors by court staff.

See also networking—Chapter 1, para **1.2.5**.

11.5   Establishing and maintaining high standard of client care

11.5.1   Your availability

In the early years you may have to be prepared to open on Saturday mornings or one evening after office hours to enable your clients to see you at a time that they can conveniently manage. Some practices offer advice shops when one or two hours' legal advice is given free.

Be careful, however, that this is not abused by clients who could easily pay for your services.

If you are unavailable to see a new client yourself it can be a good idea for your secretary to ask him to leave a document, eg a court summons, behind for you to look at when he is making a later appointment—he is then more likely to return!

Be sure not to make appointments that you are then unable to keep—this is particularly important with new clients. It is a mistake to overload your diary so that you cannot cope. If a change is unavoidable, do everything possible to rearrange to suit the client's convenience.

11.5.2   Quality paperwork

Take care about presentation of work as well as quality of content; the impression a letter or document makes at first sight is very important, not only in terms of your relationship with your client but also with other professionals who may be a source of new clients. Well-produced pleadings and statements will impress not only judges but court officials who are potential sources of valuable work such as domestic violence injunctions, for the young practice.

The importance of producing well presented, high quality work cannot be over-emphasised; the business will not succeed without it. You cannot afford to make mistakes such as misspelling the client's name or sending a letter to the wrong address. Remember that a good secretary generally costs no more than a bad one. If your first secretary is not good enough, be prepared to make a change quickly.

11.5.3   Client care generally

See Chapter 2.

11.6   Fulfilling criteria for a LAB franchise.

There are very specific criteria for applying for a LAB franchise. These are largely based on maintaining efficient management schemes and the provision of quality service to the client. It is, however, beyond the scope of this book to deal with them here. Have in mind also the Law Society management and professional standards.

DEVELOPING AN EXISTING PRACTICE

11.7 Staff

11.7.1 Efficient use of staff

In order to ensure that costs are not wasted it is important that work is delegated where appropriate to a more junior member of the department, but in each case you should consider what is right for a particular client, bearing in mind the client's expectations and ability to pay. Where there is delegation there must always be very careful supervision.

11.7.2 Structuring the department

In developing a family law department you should aim ideally for a balance of male and female personnel and for a range of staff working at different levels of experience. This will ensure your capability to deal with the widest client base and to deal with each case most cost-efficiently. There are undoubtedly some clients who are clear that they wish to be represented by one and not the other and if this cannot be offered then some clients may choose to go elsewhere.

Bear in mind also the need to have a balance of various skills within the department; to have some who, if required, are prepared to take a more 'back room' role or to be more extrovert.

The ratio of fee earners to partners tends to be low in family law work not least because much of the work may be negotiation which is hard to delegate. By way of broad generalisation a partner may have between one and three assistants.

11.7.3 Staff care

To produce quality work requires quality staff. There will usually be a level of commitment in those who choose to work in a family law department at whatever level, but this commitment needs to be nurtured and not taken for granted. Involve them where possible in decision making and planning. Hold regular departmental meetings to discuss the work.

Appraisal and performance review: carry out regular staff

appraisals. This may include a self-appraisal, and may be written, formal or informal (note the franchising requirement here).

If you are not satisfied with a member of staff's performance, then you should discuss this with him. If there is no improvement, make a change. It is always easier to tackle a problem of this nature at an early stage, rather than letting the matter drag on.

Training: offer training at all levels. It is very useful to have an office manual which covers all basic procedures. The Law Society produces a standard manual which can be adapted to suit your firm's particular requirements.

Support: be accessible to your staff at all reasonable times. Be open to their needs and problems. Be aware of stress in staff and offer help where necessary. Remember that whereas you can hand on work which you do not wish to deal with either because you are not sure how to do it, you think it will take more time than you have or because you have a poor relationship with the client, a more junior member of your team may not have that option available. Always make time to deal with your staff's questions and work problems.

See also Chapter 1.

11.7.4 Limiting the amount of work

It is extremely difficult in view of the varying complexity of each case and the wide divergence between types of firm to give even a broad indication of the size of case load each person in a department might be expected to carry. What is important, however, is to be able to recognise when you have sufficient work and that you may have to turn new work away so that existing work does not suffer. This can be very difficult after the years of establishing a practice when all work was enthusiastically received. You should, however, look upon it as a sign of success and an opportunity to be more selective about the cases you take on, thus improving the quality of your practice. It is probably worth taking on any client recommended to you by a professional colleague, particularly a referral of quality work, eg from a child psychiatrist. You will need to develop a system to filter potential new clients and it is good practice, if you are unable to take on a client, to refer him to another solicitor. If possible, try to speak to him yourself—often a client will try to come back, sometimes years later.

11.8 Systems

11.8.1 Personal systems

You will need to have your own and departmental systems to ensure that the work is handled efficiently and that mistakes are not made (*see* Chapter 1, para **1.3**).

11.8.2 Computer systems

Computer systems are undoubtedly a very helpful tool in the running of a successful family law department, whether for accounting or for word processing. Remember, however, that the information provided by an accounting system is merely one tool of management not to be over-relied upon. By way of an obvious example, low billing figures by one assistant for one month do not necessarily mean that that assistant is not working hard enough.

Word processing packages can save a great deal of time and the expense of buying printed forms but beware of overuse at the expense of relevance, eg do not try to produce a standardised r 2.63 FPR 1991 questionnaire.

11.9 Costs

11.9.1 Charging rates

In order to establish a sensible charging rate you need first of all to calculate the expense of time using the Law Society's formula. You should then find out what other firms in your locality are charging and what rates the court will allow. Then look at what you need to make a profit and finally consider what your clients can afford.

11.9.2 Billing

However successful a case you run, you will not be doing yourself, your firm, or indeed the client, any service if the question of payment of costs is not clearly addressed throughout the case.

Efficient time recording is an essential element in proper charging and billing. When the expense of time is calculated (see *above*) assumptions will be made on the number of working hours in a year. Make sure that you and your staff are achieving those hours and that they are being billed against the client. It is important that time recorded on files corresponds with time recorded on the firm's accounting system and that it is a fair reflection of the time spent. On taxation the court will need to see the details recorded on the file.

As to explaining charging rates to the client and asking for money on account, *see* Chapter 2, para **2.3.9**.

Submit interim bills as often as you can—a computerised accounting system can be helpful for this. Remember, however, that no-one likes paying for family work, and that it is important to time your bills carefully, eg after the preparation of an affidavit, or after *decree nisi*, so that the client feels that something positive has been achieved.

11.9.3 Unpaid bills

It is important, too, to follow up debts, adopting the line that just as the client expects you to be business-like about his affairs, so he should expect you to be business-like about your own. Encourage your staff to have a similarly robust attitude to the payment of bills. As a junior member of staff, beware of the senior partner's pet client who cannot be billed and make sure that the responsibility for this is placed where it lies.

Work out a procedure to be followed, perhaps involving a personal telephone call in the first instance, followed by a couple of written reminders. If it becomes necessary to sue, it is often sensible to hand the file to another member of the firm to deal with. Be prepared to be flexible in those cases where it is clearly difficult for your client to meet the bill—agree payment by instalments if necessary. In some cases it may be possible to get the other party to pay.

11.10 Marketing

11.10.1 Most common sources of new clients

Where the firm is centrally based in a large city, clients do not tend to walk in off the street. In such practices the most important source of new clients is likely to be recommendations by former clients and by other professionals, usually other solicitors or counsel.

11.10.2 Advertising

Advertising is not particularly helpful for a city-located firm, but specifically targeted PR may be, eg through distribution to other professionals of brochures containing information about either the firm's/department's practice or a topical issue, eg Child Support Act 1991, or the holding of an appropriate seminar or lecture.

For a smaller practice it may be useful to distribute brochures or newsletters printed by the Law Society which deal with specific areas of law such as divorce, wills, and which can be ordered with the firm's name printed on them.

Think very carefully before employing professional PR assistance, as it is likely to be a costly exercise. Work out where new clients are likely to come from and do not waste resources in pursuing unproductive areas.

11.10.3   Maintaining your own and your department's · profile

(*See above*, para **11.4.3**)

It is important not only to maintain a high profile amongst other professionals in your own field but also in other areas of law. Do not neglect to remind other partners in your own firm of the services your department has to offer to their existing clients.

11.11   Relationship between family law department and rest of firm

11.11.1   Justifying your existence

There is sometimes a need in a large practice, particularly one which is commercially oriented, to justify the existence of a family law department where, by virtue of the nature of the work and the fact that the client must pay from his own resources, profits may not be as substantial as in other areas.

Remind your other partners that not only does family work appear set to increase in quantity but that the family law client is a good source of other related work, such as conveyancing, drafting a new will, and tax planning. Family law clients tend to remain loyal to a firm that has handled their case well, partly, no doubt, because of the bond established between the client and the solicitor in the course of dealing with an intensely personal matter. Point out also the danger of existing clients of other departments having to look elsewhere for advice on matrimonial matters and the possibility of them being lured away from the firm altogether. Target your marketing to make your department appear invaluable to the other partners of the firm.

11.11.2 Establishing/expanding a family law department in an existing firm

All that is said above applies. Support your arguments on the benefit to existing clients and the benefit to other departments with a well-researched business plan.

11.12 Planning for the future

11.12.1 Regular assessment

Plans for the future, be they short-term or long-term, must be based on what has gone before. You will need regular updates on the amount of work in progress, unbilled work, chargeable hours, unpaid bills, office overheads. Computerisation will assist, but in a small firm may not be as necessary because you will be more in touch with what is happening with manual management information. However, do not rely on your own memory and impressions. Good and accessible record keeping is essential.

11.12.2 Long-term planning

Long-term planning will include reviewing the profitability of the department and isolating areas for improvement, considering career planning for existing staff, the number of staff likely to be required, areas of practice to develop. Drawing up business plans periodically can assist in clarifying issues and identifying strengths and weaknesses, as well as planning for the future.

You will also wish to give consideration as to whether existing areas of speciality within the department should be expanded and to how proposed changes in the law may affect the nature of the business and how such opportunities can be met. For example, joining the SFLA will keep you aware of what is happening in family law. Read *Family Law* and the *Law Society's Gazette* and other more general periodicals such as the *Solicitor's Journal*, etc.

Appendices

1 Useful works of reference
2 Instructions in family proceedings
3 Bereavement graph
4 Referral agencies
5 Precedent letter to valuer
6 Precedent letter of instruction to actuary re pension and FPR 2.63 questionnaire
7 Guidelines for use by solicitors in the conduct of ancillary relief claims and Practice Note in *Evans*
8 Example of domestic violence checklist
9 Precedent letter explaining legal aid

Appendix 1 Useful works of reference

Bird	Child Maintenance: The Child Support Act 1991 (2nd edn), Family Law, 1993
Burrows	The Child Support Act 1991—A Practitioner's Guide, Butterworths, 1993
——	Civil Legal Aid—A Practical Guide, Plymbridge, 1989
Butterworths	Family Law Service, Butterworths, looseleaf
Clarke, Parker and Blair	*Practical Matrimonial Precedents, Longman, looseleaf
Clarke Hall and Morrison	Law Relating to Children, Butterworths, looseleaf
CPAG	The National Welfare Benefits Handbook CPAG, 1993
——	The Rights Guide to Non-means Tested Benefits CPAG, 1993
Ellison	Pensions in Divorce, Pensions Management Institute, 1991
Family Law	*Family Court Practice, Family Law, 1993
Feldman, Linda	Child Protection Law, Longman, 1992
FLBA	*At a Glance, FLBA, 1993
Fricker	Family Courts: Emergency Remedies and Procedures (2nd edn), Family Law, 1993
Hershman and MacFarlane	Children: Law and Practice, Jordans, looseleaf
Jackson and Davies	Matrimonial Finance and Taxation (5th edn), Butterworths, 1992
Law Society	*Guide to the Professional Conduct of Solicitors (6th edn), Law Society, 1993
Legal Aid Board	Legal Aid Handbook 1993, Sweet & Maxwell, 1993
Mostyn	Child's Pay (book and computer program), FLBA, 1993
Rayden and Jackson	*Law and Practice in Divorce and Family Matters (16th edn), SFLA, 1990
Salter	Pension and Insurance on Family Breakdown, Family Law, 1992
SFLA	*Precedents for Consent Orders (3rd edn), SFLA, 1990
——	Guide to Family Law in Europe, SFLA, looseleaf
Tolley	Income Tax 1993–94, Tolley, 1993
——	Capital Gains Tax 1993–94, Tolley, 1993
Wylie	Taxation of Husband and Wife: The New Rules, Butterworths, 1991

(Texts marked * are essential)

Appendix 2 Instructions in family proceedings

Client:
Full Name: _____
Address: _____
_____
_____

Telephone No: Home: _____ Work: _____
Occupation: _____
Name and Address of Employers: _____
_____
_____
Date of Birth: _____

Spouse/Cohabitee:
Full Name: _____
Address: _____
_____
_____

Occupation: _____
Name and Address of Employers: _____
_____

Date of Birth: _____

Marriage:
DATE: _____
Place: _____
Status at marriage: Wife: _____ Husband: _____
Wife's maiden/former name: _____
Location of marriage certificate: _____
Religion: _____
Address of last Cohabitation Last date: _____
_____
_____
_____

Previous Proceedings:
Nature: _____
Previous Solicitors _____
Client: _____   Spouse/Cohabitee: _____

_____   _____
_____   _____

Matrimonial Home
Address _____

_____
_____

In whose name is it?

If owned:

(a)   date of purchase
(b)   purchase price
(c)   how financed (how much contributed by each/mortgage/home loan?)
(d)   present estimated value
(e)   date of original mortgage/home loan
(f)   what is outstanding mortgage balance?
(g)   do you have repayment mortgage/home loan? If so, what are the monthly capital repayments, excluding arrears? Who pays?
(h)   do you have endowment mortgage/home loan? If so, what are the monthly endowment premiums, excluding arrears? Who pays?
(i)   what type of endowment policy do you have (term assurance/low cost endowment/full cost (with profit) endowment/other)? Name of company
(j)   do you have a pension mortgage? Details of payments.
(k)   do you have a second mortgage/home loan? If so, please provide details listed above in questions (e)–(i).

If rented:

(a)   amount paid weekly/monthly?
(b)   does rent include an amount for services? If so, how much is included and for what services?

Annual Income: Client

(a)   Salary (gross before tax and national insurance)

(b) net salary
     Bonus or commission in last year
     Perks – company car
             – medical insurance
             – luncheon vouchers
             – other (please specify)

(c) *If self employed* profit share and/or drawings for each of last three years

(d) *Other Income*   *Gross*   *Net*
     pension
     casual earnings
     bank/building
     society interest
     Dividends/
     investment income
     rental income
     trust income
     child benefit
     one parent
     benefit
     other (please specify)

Annual Income: Spouse

(a) Salary (gross before tax and national insurance)

(b) net salary
     Bonus or commission in last year
     Perks – company car
              – medical insurance
             – luncheon vouchers
             – other (please specify)

(c) *If self employed* profit share and/or drawings for each of last three years

(d) *Other Income*   *Gross*   *Net*
     pension
     casual earnings
     bank/building
     society interest
     Dividends/
     investment income
     rental income
     trust income
     child benefit
     one parent
     benefit
     other (please specify)

Capital

1 *Real Property*

Please list any real property (other than your matrimonial home) in your sole name or held jointly with your husband/wife or anyone else together with details of its approximate value and full details of all outstanding mortgages or charges over the property (in particular supplying the amount of the outstanding mortgage or charge and the name of the Building Society or Bank in each case).

2 *Life Assurance Policies*

Please give full details of all Life Assurance Policies held, eg whether on sole or joint lives, the total amount assured, the duration, and the present surrender value. Please state in the case of each policy (ie assigned to a Bank or Building Society as security for a mortgage or charge).

3 *Stocks, Shares and Securities*

Please give full details of all shares held including number of shares, company in which they are held and approximate present value. Similar details should be given for all other securities and investments and share option schemes. If they are unrealisable before a certain date without tax or other penalties (eg BES investments), this fact should be stated and the relevant date given. Please state whether the shares/investments are held in your sole name or joint names with your husband/wife or anyone else.

4 *Building Society and Bank Accounts*

Please give full details of all Building Society and Bank accounts held, including the name of the Bank or Building Society, the branch, the nature of the account, the number of the account and the current balance in the account. Please confirm whether the accounts are in your sole name or held jointly with your husband/wife or anyone else.

5 *Other Assets*

Please give details in full as per above of any other capital assets owned by you, either solely or jointly with your husband/wife or anyone else. This should include, eg premium bonds/cars/boats/jewellery/paintings/antiques and other valuable contents.

Liabilities

Please give full details of all outstanding liabilities which are not covered above. For instance, mortgages and Bank overdrafts should be included in the details given above but any other outstanding liabilities, such as, for instance, large amounts outstanding on credit cards, tax bills, etc should be included here. You should also include, if applicable, an estimate of any Capital Gains Tax liability you may incur in relation to the disposal of any of the assets listed above.

Pension Arrangements

Please give full details of all pension arrangements you have made, including, in particular, up-to-date valuations and full details of the benefits likely to be available to you under your pension schemes on retirement. Documentary evidence of these should be made available.

Outgoings

Please give full details of regular monthly outgoings as per attached Proforma Statement.

List of Outgoings

Please supply approximate monthly figures in each case.

Accommodation Expenses	*Per month* £
Mortgage	
Rent	
Ground Rent	
Service Charge	
Council Tax	
Water Rates	
Gas	
Electricity	
Fuel (Coal/Oil etc)*	
Telephone	
House Insurance	
Contents Insurance	
Repairs/Maintenance	
Cleaner	
Gardener/Garden Equipment*	
and Expenses	
Window Cleaner	
Sub totals	£

*Please delete items which are not applicable

General living expenses   £

Food
General Household items
Clothes
Laundry/Dry cleaning
Car Insurance
Car repairs and Maintenance
Car tax
Petrol/diesel*
AA/RAC subscription*
Fares to work/season ticket
HP Payments
Life assurance premiums
Pension contributions
Private medical insurance premiums
Dental treatment/Spectacles/Contact lenses*
Medicines/prescriptions
Hairdresser
Entertainment (theatres, concerts etc)
TV Licence
TV/Video Rental*
Holidays
Christmas
Pet food/vet's bills etc
Newspapers and magazines
Subscriptions (please specify)
Miscellaneous (please specify)

    TOTALS

*Please delete items which are not applicable

Expenditure on child(ren)   £

Food
Clothes
Petrol
Private medical insurance premiums
Medicines/toiletries
Hairdresser
Nanny (and related expenses)
Outings for entertainment
Presents (and for children to take to parties)*

Expenditure on child(ren)—contd £

Babysitter/Childminder
School fees
School meals
Pocket money
Holidays
Subscriptions (please specify)
Miscellaneous (please specify)   ————————

   TOTAL   ════════

*Please delete items which are not applicable

Children

1 *Children of both parties*

Full name   *Date of Birth*

2 *Other children of the family* (ie children of either party who have been treated as children of the family). Please give full names, dates of birth and relationship to you and your husband/wife. In the case of stepchildren, please give father's name and address and details of financial contributions made to the children, whether voluntary or by court order.

3 *Other children who are not children of the family* (ie born to you or your husband/wife but neither treated by you as children of the family nor adopted by you both). Please give same details as in 2.

4 *Accommodation occupied by children listed under 1 and 2 above:*
(a) addresses.
(b) number of living rooms and bedrooms.
(c) is house rented or owned and by whom?
     is rent/mortgage paid regularly?
(d) Names of all other persons living with children and relationship to them.

5 *Education*

Names of school/college attended and whether these are fee-paying. Who pays fees and how much are they?
Do children have any special educational needs? If so please specify.

6 *Childcare Details*

If parent with day-to-day care works please give details of hours worked and of who looks after children while parent is not there.

7 *Health*

Are children in good health? If not, please give details of any special health needs and names of GP/Consultant.

8 *Maintenance*

Does husband/wife pay towards children's upkeep? Details please.

9 *Contact arrangements*

(Note—essential to ascertain exact number of nights children spend with 'absent parents' in all cases where there is extensive staying contact or shared care arrangements.)

10 *Details of care or any other court proceedings other than Child Support Agency applications.*

11 Would you agree to see a conciliator if there were difficulties with respect to the arrangements for the children?

12 Do the children have any income, earned or unearned, or capital? Please provide full details of amounts and source of income.

13 *Child support Act checklist—basic information required (if not already obtained):*

Children
(a) What are the names and dates of birth of the children?
(b) How many nights per week do the children spend with each parent on average?
(c) Are there any existing maintenance orders in force in respect of the children?

Parents
In respect of each parent:
(a) Do the parents live alone or with someone else?
(b) What is the relationship of the parent with that person?
(c) Does that person make any contribution to that parent's housing costs? If so, provide details of that person's age and their gross weekly income.

Income
In respect of each parent and each partner:
(a) Provide the net and gross figures for *all* sources of income (for example, salary, bonus, stocks and shares, building society);
(b) What are the pension contributions of each parent?

Housing
In respect of each parent:
(a) Provide details of the amount of rent/mortgage repayments made and the period of payment.
(b) Apportion the mortgage repayments between interest/capital and endowment premiums, or give best estimate.
(c) What is the current interest rate applicable to the mortgage?

Appendix 3 Bereavement graph

Reactions to loss*

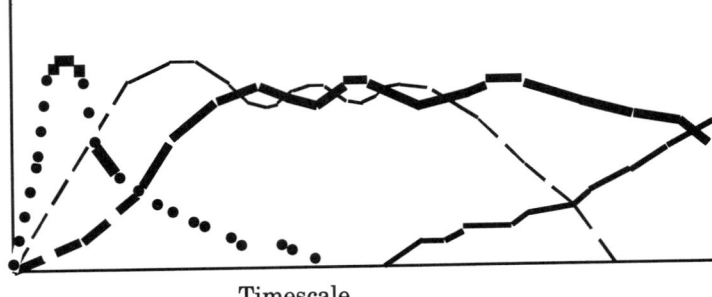

Degree of Reaction

Timescale

Four phases of mourning
Denial, numbness
Pining, anger, depression
Disorganisation and despair
Reorganisation and recovery

*Graph produced by Christopher Clulow of the Tavistock Institute of Marital Studies based on the work of Colin Murray Parkes in *Bereavement: Studies of Grief in Adult Life* (2nd edn), Harmondsworth, Penguin, 1983.

Appendix 4   Referral agencies

Solicitors Family Law Association (SFLA)
Mrs MI'Anson
PO Box 302
Keston
Kent, BR2 6EZ
tel. 0689 850227

Counselling

ADR Family Register
tel. 0800 616130

Family Mediators Association (FMA)
Mrs Lisa Parkinson
The Old House
Rectory Gardens
Henbury
Bristol BS10 7AQ
tel. 0272 500141

or

Mrs Jacqueline Klarfeld
c/o 1 Old Forge Close
Stanmore
Middlesex HA7 3EB
tel. 081–954 6383

Institute of Family Therapy
43 New Cavendish Street
London W1M 7RG
tel. 071–935 1651

National Association of Mediation and Conciliation Services (NAFMACS)
The Shaftesbury Centre
Percy Street, Wiltshire
Swindon SN2 2AZ
tel. 0793 514055
(and local affiliated services)

Relate
Herbert Gray College
Little Church Street
Rugby CV21 3AP
tel. 0788 573241

Tavistock Institute of Marital Studies
120 Belsize Lane
London NW3 5BA
tel. 071–435 7111

Organisations running telephone helplines

Childline
tel. 0800 1111

Children's Legal Centre
20 Compton Terrace
London N1 2UN
tel. 071–359 6251 (helpline)

Exploring Parenthood
Latimer Education Centre
194 Freston Road
London W10 6TT
tel. 081–960 1678

Family Rights Group (FRG)
6-9 Manor Gardens
Holloway Road
London N7 6LA
tel. 071–272 7308

National Children's Bureau
8 Wakeley Street
London EC1V 7QE
tel. 071–278 9441

Rape Crisis Centre
PO Box 69
London WC1X 9NJ
tel. 071–278 3956 (office) and 071–837 1600 (24 hrs)

Step Family
72 Willesden Lane
London NW6
tel. 071–372 0844 (enquiries) and 071–372 0846 (helpline)

Other organisations

Alcoholics (Al-Anon for Relatives)
61 Great Dover Sreet
London SE1 4YF
tel. 071–403 0888

Catholic Marriage Advisory Council
23 Kensington Square
London W8 5HN
tel. 071–937 3781

Council of Sharia
34 Francis Road
London E10
tel. 081–889 6662

Families Need Fathers
10 Hartley Close
Bromley
Kent BR1 2TP
tel. 081–295 1956 or 071–613 5060 (London)

Gingerbread Association for One Parent Families
35 Wellington Street
London WC2E 7BN
tel. 071–240 0935

Jewish Marriage Council
23 Ravenhurst Avenue
London NW4 4EE
tel. 081–203 6311

Joint Council for The Welfare of Immigrants (JCWI)
115 Old Street
London EC1V 9JR
tel. 071–251 8706

International Academy of Matrimonial Lawyers
Jeremy Levison, (secretary)
Messrs Collyer Bristow,
4 Bedford Row,
London WC1
tel. 071–242 7363

REUNITE National Council for Abducted Children
PO Box 4
London WC1
tel. 071–404 8356

Women's Aid Federation
Unit Cheene Court
Cheene
Bristol B53 4AG
tel. 0272 633494 and 0272 633 542 (helpline)

Useful local numbers to know

Samaritans
Police Domestic Violence Unit
Citizens Advice Bureaux
Cultural organisations
Child Support Agency helpline

Appendix 5   Precedent letter to valuer

Messrs

Surveyors and valuers

Dear Sirs,

Re [address]

We represent Mr B in connection with his matrimonial proceedings and Messrs   are representing Mrs B. We are writing jointly with Mrs B's solicitors to ask you to carry out a valuation of (property) on behalf of Mr and Mrs B.

Please provide a formal valuation of the property on the basis that it is an open market value, namely the best price at which a sale might reasonably be expected to have been completed for a cash consideration on the date of the valuation assuming;

(a)   a willing seller

(b)   that prior to the valuation there has been a reasonable period for the marketing

(c)   that the state of the market, levels of values and other circumstances remain constant during the period of the marketing.

We also seek your opinion upon the following matters;

(here set out any other matters, such as a sale by lot, or application for planning permission, or income possibilities, or any other relevant matter and also specifically state if a structural survey is required as this is not required for a formal valuation unless specifically requested).

Before commencing this valuation, we would be grateful if you would let us have an estimate of how long you are likely to need in preparing the report, together with details of your charging rates and the way in which the cost of your report will be calculated. On the subject of costs, although Mr and Mrs B are instructing you jointly, Mr B has agreed to meet the entire costs of the report and your account should therefore be made out to him care of us. (Or 'as Mr and Mrs B are instructing you jointly they have agreed to pay your account equally and so please send each of them an account for one half care of our respective firms.')

If you have any enquiries we should be grateful if you would address them to Mr B   at this firm (Mr B's solicitor) or Mrs B   at (Mrs B's solicitor).

We look forward to hearing from you.

Yours faithfully,

Appendix 6 Precedent letter of instruction to actuary re pension and FPR 2.63 questionnaire*

Our Ref

Dear Sirs

1   We act for the person named below in divorce proceedings whose spouse is a member of the pension arrangements mentioned below.

2   We would be grateful for your opinion as to the value of the following losses which would be suffered by our client following a decree absolute of divorce as at ( ):[1]

    loss of survivor's pension

    loss of interest in the spouse's pension

    loss of interest in death benefits.

3   We enclose[2]

    copy of the trust deed, including the rules of the scheme[3]

    copy of the explanatory booklet relating to the scheme

    information provided by the spouse's solicitors

    copy of the questionnaire served on the spouse's solicitors[4]

    copy of the latest annual benefit statement of the spouse

4   We set out below some information which you will require:

    Name of client in full (m/f) dob

    Name of spouse in full (m/f) dob

    Name of occupational pension scheme

    Date of marriage

    Names of children and dob

    1

    2

    3

    Spouse's salary

    Spouse's pensionable salary[5]

    Spouse's date of commencement of employment

    Spouse's date of joining scheme (if different)

    Spouse's unfunded pension arrangements[6]

5   Please let us know if you require any further information, and let us have an estimate of your charges before undertaking your valuation.

Yours faithfully

*First published in the *Gazette* and reproduced with the kind permission of The Law Society.

Notes

You will need to give separate details of each occupational pension scheme involved as the spouse may have pension arrangements with a series of occupational schemes. This letter is not designed to cater for personal pension contracts.

You can find a consulting actuary by writing to the Association of Consulting Actuaries, 1 Wardrobe Place, London EC4V 5AH: tel. 071 248 3163. In the case of insured pension arrangements (and for that matter all other pension arrangements) failure to disclose the required information in a reasonable time can be resolved either by use of the Occupational Pension Schemes (Disclosure of Information) Regulations 1986 (SI 86/1046) as amended by SI 86/1717 or, where this is not appropriate, by serving a notice on the pensions manager or insurance company under r 2.62(7) of the Family Proceedings Rules 1991 for them to attend on a 'production appointment'.

This document is not appropriate for state pension benefits. You can obtain information about state benefits by sending form BR19 to the Department of Social Security, RPFA Unit, Room 37D, Central Office, Newcastle Upon Tyne NE96 17X.

Footnotes

1   Please tick as appropriate—in most cases all this information will be required. The date given will usually be the date of the ancillary relief hearing although in some cases it may be appropriate to ask for the rights to be valued at a future date such as the normal retirement date.
2   Please tick as appropriate.
3   This is not usually necessary if the up-to-date explanatory booklet is available.
4   *See* pensions questionnaire *below* under r 2.63 of the Family Proceedings Rules 1991 approved by the family law committee.
5   You should state where this information comes from, ie from a P60, contract of employment or bonus statement (whether including taxable share options).
6   Details of any special terms include pension rights or expectations (ie non-formalised or unfunded) which may be contained, for example, in the contract of employment or a side-letter, rather than in the pension scheme. Unfunded arrangements should be specifically mentioned, as should the risk of non-payment of such pensions.

The pensions questionnaire

This questionnaire is approved by the Law Society's family law committee and designed to comply with r 2.63 of the Family Proceedings Rules 1991.

Please provide the following information relating to any pension rights or expectations in connection with the petitioner/respondent.

1 Name of petitioner/respondent.
2 Name of scheme(s)[1].
3 Copies of trust deed and rules of the scheme[2]; explanatory booklet; benefit statement (not more than 12 months old); trustees' annual report (latest); notes of any material changes to this information.
4 Details of transfers in from other schemes.
5 Details of any special terms agreed with the employer not contained in information supplied above[3].
6 Details of any additional voluntary contributions payable by the petitioner/respondent and of the nature of the benefits secured thereby.
7 Is the petitioner/respondent contracted out of the earnings related part of the state pension scheme by virtue of his or her membership of the scheme?
8 Details of the trustees'/ employer's policy regarding guaranteed/discretionary increases. In the case of discretionary increases please supply a statement of practice or details of the increases granted in the recent past.
9 Normal retirement age[4].
10 Statement from the trustees of each scheme (or other appropriate source) explaining and quantifying the projected benefits—on the basis that contributions continue at the present rate until retirement; and—on the basis that no further contributions are made in relation to:
   (a) lump sum payable in the event of death in service;
   (b) spouse's pension payable in the event of death in service;
   (c) the pension which the petitioner/respondent will receive upon retirement at normal retirement age on the basis that s/he does not elect to commute part of his/her pension for a lump sum;
   (d) the maximum lump sum which the petitioner/respondent could receive in part commutation of his/her pension;
   (e) the maximum pension payable from normal retirement date in the event of such commutation; and
   (f) spouse's pension on death after retirement.
11 Statement of current transfer value[5].
12 Details of current medical conditions which might affect the value of rights under scheme.

Notes

Most of this information can be legally required to be provided to members of schemes and their spouses under the disclosure regulations (Occupational Pension Schemes (Disclosure of Information) Regulations 1986 (SI 86/1046) as amended by (SI 86/1717)).

This questionnaire should not be sent as a matter of course; it is appropriate only where, at the date of the hearing, there is a reasonable expectation of significant pension losses, for instance, loss of an enforceable widow's pension, where a return of premiums on death is possible, where the parties have been married for some time, where the respondent is in pensionable employment and is nearing retirement, and where the salary is significant (or in the public sector where pensions are significant in relation to earnings).

If the marriage is long-lasting, even lower paid spouses should be asked to complete the questionnaire; even a modest pension which cannot be settled by an adjustment of the other matrimonial property could be enough to hold up a *decree nisi*. This applies particularly to pensions in the public sector (see eg *Parkes* v *Parkes*) [1971] 1 WLR 1481; *Le Marchant* v *Le Marchant* [1977] 3 All ER 610).

Footnotes

1   A separate questionnaire should be simultaneously completed for each pension arrangement involved.
2   All these documents must be supplied by law by the pension provider or trustees.
3   Details of any special terms include pension rights or expectations (ie non-formalised or unfunded) which may be contained for example in the contract of employment or a side-letter, rather than in the pension scheme. Unfunded arrangements should be specifically mentioned, as should the risk of non-payment of such pensions.
4   Normal retirement age is the age set down in the pension scheme; it should be the same as the contract of employment.
5   Current transfer value should be calculated on the basis of cash equivalents under the transfer regulations.

Appendix 7 Guidelines for use by solicitors in the conduct of ancillary relief claims* and Practice Note in *Evans*

Section 1—The SFLA Code of Practice

General

1.1 The solicitor should endeavour to advise, negotiate and conduct proceedings in a manner calculated to encourage and assist the parties to achieve a constructive settlement of their differences as quickly as may be reasonable whilst recognising that the parties may need time to come to terms with their new situation and should inform the client of the approach he intends to adopt.

1.2 The solicitor should treat his work in relation to the children as the most important of his duties. The solicitor should encourage the client to see the advantages to the family of a non-litigious approach as a way of resolving their disputes. The solicitor should explain to the client that in cases where there are children the attitude of the client to the other parent in any negotiations will affect the family as a whole and may affect the relationship of the children with the parents.

1.3 The solicitor should encourage the attitude that a family dispute is not a contest in which there is one winner and one loser, but rather a search for fair solutions. He should avoid using words or phrases that imply a dispute when no serious dispute necessarily exists, for example 'opponent', 'win', 'lose', or *Smith* v *Smith*.

1.4 Because of the involvement of personal emotions in family disputes the solicitor should where possible avoid heightening such emotions by the advice given; and by avoiding expressing opinions as to the behaviour of the other party.

1.5 The solicitor should also have regard to the impact of correspondence on the other party when writing a letter of which a copy may be sent to that party and should also consider carefully the impact of correspondence on his own client before sending copies of letters to the client.

1.6 The solicitor should aim to avoid or dispel suspicion or mistrust between parties, by encouraging at an early stage where possible, full frank and clear disclosure of information and openness in dealings.

*Reproduced with the kind permission of the SFLA.

Relationship with client

2.1   As a rule the solicitor should explain to the client at the outset the terms of his retainer and take care to ensure that the client is fully aware of the impact of costs on any chosen course of action. The solicitor should thereafter at all stages have regard to the cost of negotiations and proceedings.

2.2   Where appropriate, the solicitor must advise the client of his right to apply for legal aid. He should bear in mind and explain the impact of costs where the client or the other party is in receipt of legal aid, and the particular effect of the statutory charge.

2.3   The solicitor should create and maintain a relationship with his or her client of a kind which will preserve fully his independent judgement and avoid becoming so involved in the case that his own personal emotions may cloud his judgement.

2.4   Whilst recognising the need to advise firmly and guide the client the solicitor should ensure that where the decision is properly that of the client, it is taken by the client and that its consequences are fully understood, both as to its effect on any children involved and financially.

Dealings with other solicitors

3.1   The solicitor should in all dealings with other solicitors show courtesy and where possible endeavour to create and maintain a friendly relationship.

3.2   The solicitor should seek wherever possible to foster in his own client a trust in the other party's solicitors so tending to reduce the distrust and suspicion between the parties.

3.3   The solicitor should in financial negotiations make use of without prejudice discussions, that is to say discussions involving conditional offers and conditional admissions that are withdrawn and not disclosed to the Court in the event of those negotiations failing. The solicitor should be mindful that an unrealistic offer may be counterproductive and delay settlement.

Dealings with the other party in person

4.1   In dealings with another party who is not legally represented the solicitor should take particular care to be courteous and restrained. Especial care should be taken to express letters and other communications clearly, avoiding technical language where it is not readily understandable to the layman or might be misunderstood.

4.2   Wherever proceedings are taken or negotiations conducted that may adversely affect the other party's interests, the other party should, in the interests of both parties, be advised to consult a solicitor.

Petitions and proceedings

5.1 The solicitor should avoid allegations or procedures which may cause or increase ill-will between the parties without producing any benefit for the client.

5.2 Before instituting proceedings which make allegations about the other party's conduct, the solicitor should consider whether the other party or his solicitor should be consulted in advance as to the particulars to be alleged or the grounds to be relied on.

5.3 Where the purpose of taking a particular step in proceedings may be misunderstood the solicitor should consider explaining it in advance to the other party or his solicitors.

Children

6.1 The solicitor should, in advising, negotiating and conducting proceedings, assist both his client and the other parent to regard the welfare of the child as the first and paramount consideration.

6.2 The solicitor should aim to promote co-operation between parents in all decisions concerning the child both by formal arrangements (such as orders for joint custody); by practical arrangements (such as shared involvement in school events) and by consultation on important questions.

6.3 The solicitor must keep in mind that the interests of the child do not necessarily coincide with the interests of either parent, and that occasionally the child should be separately represented. In such case his duty is to bring the matter to the attention of the court.

6.4 The solicitor should take care to keep separate issues of custody and access on the one hand and money on the other. It is often helpful to deal with these two topics in separate letters.

6.5 'Kidnapping' of children both results from and creates exceptional fear, bitterness and desperation in the parents. The solicitor should therefore take what steps he properly can to prevent the kidnapping of a child and inform his client that he may be committing a criminal offence punishable by imprisonment.

The guidelines set out in this Code cannot be absolute rules in as much as the solicitor may have to depart from them if the law or his professional obligations so require. They are a restatement of principles, objectives and recommendations which many solicitors practising family law already seek to follow and to which they seek to aspire in serving their clients.

Section 2—Additional Guidelines

General

1.1   The solicitor should consider the timing of correspondence to his client and the effect that this will have. All letters should be written using simple language. Different issues should be separated either by the use of headings or possibly by putting them in separate letters.

1.2   If the solicitor decides to instruct counsel at any stage this decision and the reasons for it should be discussed with the client. If at all possible a conference should be arranged although it must be recognised that this is sometimes impossible or undesirable—for instance where it is not possible to guarantee that the barrister conducting the conference will also conduct the case in court.

1.3   The solicitor should avoid becoming involved with issues of conduct particularly where it is conduct of a type which the court will not take into account. This approach should be explained to the client and a multiplicity of appointments, affidavits and correspondence on these issues should be avoided.

1.4   The solicitor should consider whether the case is one where referral to a mediation, conciliation or counselling service would be appropriate. If so the type of service which would be appropriate and the issues which might be covered, eg arrangements for the children and/or financial relief should be discussed with the client and with the other party or his solicitors.

1.5   The client should always be aware from the start of proceedings upon what basis costs are to be charged. Further reference should be made to section 5 dealing with costs and to the *Client Care Guide* produced in April 1991 by the Law Society.

Relationship with the client

2.1   The solicitor should (subject to the guidance in section 1) seek to provide the client with as much support as may reasonably be required during a period which is inevitably stressful for the client.

Petitions and proceedings

3.1   Consideration should be given to using good file management techniques including a method of setting out the basic facts relating to each case which can be updated when necessary. Full attendance notes should always be made.

3.2   Affidavits should be confined to the relevant facts and should not be repetitive, irrelevant or lacking in structure. If the facts are particularly complicated headings can be used. Normally each party should file one substantive affidavit. If any further affidavit is necessary it should be confined to answering serious allegations or dealing with material changes of circumstances. An affidavit in reply is a good opportunity for the respondent to make an offer of settlement. Any affidavit should be capable of standing on its own without reference to other affidavits being necessary.

3.3 Attempts should be made to agree directions and solicitors should only ask for those directions which are absolutely necessary. The directions set out below are commonly given and could be agreed between parties:

   (a) The filing of one substantive affidavit for each party (subject to 3.2).

   (b) Valuation by an agreed valuer.

   (c) Discovery within fourteen days of the filing of affidavits with inspection to follow within seven days thereafter. If discovery does not take place in this manner or is incomplete, discovery under r 77(4) (now FPR 2.63) and where possible confined to one comprehensive questionnaire each.

   (d) Courts will often require in every case that the parties attend the hearing and in cases expected to last half a day or more, for the hearing date to be fixed on the filing of certificates of readiness and time estimates.

3.4 If a directions hearing is held and a particularly complex issue is raised it may be beneficial to ask the District Judge who deals with the hearing to reserve the case to himself as this will ensure a consistent approach throughout the case.

3.5 In a substantial case it may be desirable to have a pre-trial review to define the issues, explore the possibilities of settlement and ensure the case is ready for hearing.

3.6 It is the duty of the applicant to prepare the agreed bundle of documents which should be numbered and paginated. It is preferable for the agreed bundle to be included in a ring binder. If the applicant does not prepare an agreed bundle, the respondent may prepare a bundle for agreement or a respondent's bundle. In any event, the correct number of copies should be available for the hearing.

3.7 A chronology of material facts should be prepared, agreed and made available to the court.

3.8 Care should be taken in deciding what evidence other than professional expert evidence should be called, emotive issues should be avoided and a deponent should be available for cross-examination if an order is made for his attendance.

3.9 Net effect calculations over a range of figures are also very useful for the court and in appropriate cases evidence of a party's borrowing capacity should be available (*see Newton* v *Newton* [1990] 1 FLR 33).

3.10 All professional witnesses should be advised to be careful to avoid a partisan approach and should maintain professional standards.

Children

4.1 The solicitor should, at the time a claim for ancillary relief is made, again consider with the client whether arrangements for the children's maintenance and accommodation are satisfactory before considering other issues, thus reinforcing the fact that the interests of the children should come first.

Costs

The importance of costs has been highlighted in a number of recent cases, in particular *Evans* v *Evans* [1990] 2 All ER 147. Accordingly reference to the question of costs is also made in the sections of this guidance dealing with disclosure and negotiations or offers of settlement. Further information on costs and examples of precedent letters to private fee-paying and legally aided clients are contained in the *Client Care Guide* produced by the Law Society in April 1991.

5.1 The solicitor should take care to ensure that the client is fully aware of the level of costs at any particular stage—possibly through the use of interim bills.

5.2 Entrenched positions necessitating frequent and costly court appearances should be avoided as should a level of costs out of all proportion to the available matrimonial assets.

5.3 The solicitor should bear in mind and explain to the client that the general rule that costs follow the event does not apply in matrimonial cases and that although offers of settlement may influence the court's discretion as to costs they will not govern the exercise of that discretion. (*See also* section 7 on negotiations and offers of settlement.)

5.4 Estimates of the approximate amount of the costs of each party will be required by the court and should be prepared for submission to the court at the commencement of the hearing and at any pre-trial review of the application. These estimates should differentiate between costs already and to be occurred and between standard costs and indemnity costs. (*See Practice Direction* [1988] 2 All ER 63.) Reference should also be made to Chapter 8 of *The Guide to the Professional Conduct of Solicitors* (1990).

5.5 The solicitor should explain to his client that where the parties are not legally aided any sums paid on account of costs will be added back into the parties' assets less any sum that would never be recoverable. A similar approach will be taken in relation to any future liability for costs. The court will take this approach in all cases save where the available assets of the applicant spouse are very small (*see Leadbeater* v *Leadbeater* [1985] FLR 789).

Legal aid

5.6 A client should always be advised of the availability of legal aid (*see* principle 10.02 in *The Guide to the Professional Conduct of Solicitors*).

5.7 If a client, who is entitled to legal aid, decides to instruct a solicitor on a private basis it is advisable to obtain confirmation of this decision and the reasons for it in writing.

5.8 Where the client is entitled to legal aid and decides to instruct a solicitor on that basis an application for legal aid should be sent off as soon as possible.

5.9 Information should be given to legally aided clients on the likely cost of the matter in much the same way as it is given to private fee paying clients.

In particular a client should be informed in writing at the outset of the case and at appropriate stages thereafter:

(i)   Of the effect of the statutory charge;

(ii) that even if the client loses the case he or she may still be ordered by the Court to contribute to his or her opponent's costs even though the client's costs are covered by legal aid;

(iii) that even if the client wins the opponent may not be ordered to pay the full amount of the costs and may not be capable of paying what the opponent has been ordered to pay; and

(iv) of the client's obligation to pay any contribution assessed and of the consequences of any failure to do so.

5.10 The solicitor has a duty of care to the legal aid fund and therefore should advise and act on behalf of the legally aided client in exactly the same way as for a private client and this should be explained to the client. A situation should not be manipulated to produce an artificial result at the expense of the Legal Aid Board and the solicitor should take care not to take action leading to unnecessary dissipation of the parties' assets to no good result (*see Clark* v *Clark* [1991] 1 FLR 179). To do otherwise may mean that the solicitor is out of pocket as far as deferred costs are concerned and may be the subject of a referral to the Solicitors Complaints Bureau.

5.11 The court when making an order will assume where appropriate that the Legal Aid Board will exercise its discretion to postpone enforcement of the statutory charge (*see Scallon* v *Scallon* (1990) 20 Fam Law 92).

Disclosure

6.1 The solicitor should explain to the client that a failure to make full disclosure may put the client at risk on costs (*see E* v *E* (1989) 153 JPN 772 and *W* v *W* [1989] 153 JPN 769) and may even be judged to be conduct which should be taken into account when making an order (*see*

B v *B* (1988) 18 Fam Law 435), or lead to an order for fixed costs. (*See Newton* v *Newton* [1990] 1 FLR 33.)

6.2 If the client decides, having received the solicitor's advice, that an accountant should be instructed this should be done as soon as possible and the accountant should, if necessary, be used to draft the appropriate section of the r 77 questionnaire. It should be made clear whether an accountant is to have the status of an adviser or an independent expert.

6.3 Where possible, property valuations should be obtained from a valuer jointly instructed by both parties. Where each party instructs a valuer, reports should be exchanged and if necessary the valuers should meet in an attempt to resolve differences. If possible a valuation obtained by one party should be agreed by the other party. In any event only one valuer should be instructed by each party (*see E* v *E* (1989) 153 JPN 772).

6.4 Whilst it may be necessary to obtain a broad assessment of the value of the shareholding in a private company, it is not appropriate to instruct accountants to undertake an expensive and probably meaningless exercise to achieve a precise valuation of a company which will not be sold and which will provide the income for the family in future years (*see B* v *B* [1989] 1 FLR 119) or where preliminary discovery reveals that the applicant will be able to meet any reasonable order of the court (*see B* v *B* (1990) 20 Fam Law 335). As in para 6.3 valuations should be agreed wherever possible.

6.5 In certain circumstances, however, it will be appropriate to obtain a more detailed valuation but only when the asset in question is likely to be sold (*see Moorish* v *Moorish* [1984] 14 Fam Law 26).

6.6 Setting aside for non disclosure:

An order in ancillary relief proceedings can only be set aside by lodging an appeal with a higher court or by bringing a fresh action to set it aside or by having it reheard by the same tribunal. A detailed examination of the different procedures is available in the case *B-T* v *B-T* (Divorce Procedure) [1990] 2 FLR 1.

A digest of the rules is contained in the table set out below which is based on that in the judgement in *B-T* v *B-T* (Divorce Procedure) [1990] 2 FLR 1—reference should also be made to the forthcoming Family Proceedings Rules in case any provisions amending this table exist. (*See* authors' note *below*.)

Type of order	Appeal	Fresh Action	Rehearing
1 County Court District Judge, by consent	*Yes, without leave. Fresh evidence admissible without leave. Hearing de novo. Apply within 5 days	Yes	Yes, apply to District Judge
2 High Court District Judge, by consent	**ditto Apply within 5 days in the principal registry and 7 days in the district registry	Yes	No
3 County court judge, by consent	Yes, but only with leave of the judge. Need leave of the Court of Appeal to admit fresh evidence. Apply within 4 weeks	Yes	Yes, apply to judge
4 High Court judge by consent	ditto Apply within 4 weeks	Yes	No
5 County court District Judge, after contested hearing	Yes, without leave Fresh evidence admissible. Hearing de novo. Apply within 5 days	Yes	Maybe not
6 High Court District Judge, after contested hearing	ditto to the judge Principal registry Apply within 5 days. District registry apply within 7 days	Yes	No
7 County court judge, after contested hearing	Yes, but with leave of judge or Court of Appeal. Need leave to admit fresh evidence. Apply within 4 weeks	Yes	Maybe not
8 High Court judge	ditto Apply within 4 weeks	Yes	No

Authors' note
*It appears that by virtue of FPR 1991, rr 1.3(1) and 8.1 and 2 consent orders can no longer be appealed
**Such orders may still be appealed

Negotiations and offers of settlement

7.1 The solicitor should wherever possible seek to persuade the client to settle on reasonable terms. The client should be reminded of his or her duty to negotiate. If the client upon receipt of a reasonable offer refuses to settle the action the solicitor should set out his advice that the action should be settled in writing. If the client is in receipt of legal aid it may also be appropriate to inform the Legal Aid Board that the client is acting unreasonably—the client's attention should also be drawn to this point.

7.2 The solicitor should explain to the client that an unreasonable failure to accept an offer may put the offeree at risk on costs (*see Pick* v *Pick and Nakama* (1981) 11 Fam Law 187 or *E* v *E* (1989) 153 JPN 772.

7.3 The onus is on the respondent to make an offer and failure to do so may put him at risk on costs. Where there are cross applications it may be wise for both sides to make a reasonable offer in order to protect themselves (*see Moorish* v *Moorish* (1984) 14 Fam Law 26 or *E* v *E* (1989) 153 JPN 772.

7.4 The solicitor should give careful consideration to the contents of an offer and in particular:
   (a) An offer should be comprehensive and refer to specific sums where appropriate.
   (b) It is advisable to make an offer on the basis of a clean break or otherwise as it may not be possible to predict on what basis a court will decide the issue.
   (c) Care should be taken to ensure that the offer is in terms which can be enforced by the court.
   (d) Care should be taken to ensure that all material terms (in particular costs) are covered by the offer.

7.5 A number of different modes of making an offer exist:
   (a) Without prejudice offers—these are of limited use since the advent of *Calderbank* offers although they may be of use at an early stage in negotiations as they do not bring with them the threat on costs inherent in *Calderbank* offers.
   (b) Open offers—possibly in an affidavit—these may be influential when the court is considering liabilities for costs, conduct or all the circumstances of the case.
   (c) *Calderbank* offers—in the county courts these should be sent to the other side and in addition, unlike the High Court, a copy should be filed at court in a sealed envelope.
   (d) Offers to negotiate in person.
   (e) An open offer combined with a more generous *Calderbank* offer.

7.6 An offer should not be made before an offeree has sufficient information on which to assess its reasonableness. An offer should be made at least 14 days before the hearing date and subject to the above at the earliest possible opportunity.

7.7 The solicitor should ensure that negotiations proceed in conjunction with the necessary formalities for commencing an action so that if, due to the attitude of the other party, negotiations are not achieving the hoped for results they can be curtailed. The parties will then be able to proceed to a court hearing with the minimum of delay. The solicitor/client should however remain open to further negotiations while remembering that protracted and unproductive negotiations not only waste time but increase costs probably to no effect.

Drafting consent orders

8.1 Where appropriate these should be drafted to ensure that postponement of the statutory charge is possible, ie by referring to the fact that the property is to be used as a home or a sum of money is to be used for buying a home. The consent order should refer to the Act under which it is made. (It is believed that a Practice Direction on this point may be forthcoming—if so reference should be made to it).

8.2 The solicitor should ensure that the statement of information under r 76A is comprehensive—in particular details of capital and net income should be shown as at the date of the statement. The statement should also include details of the net equity of any property and the effect of its proposed distribution (*see Registrar's Direction* (1990) 20 Fam Law 112).

8.3 In drafting a consent order the solicitor should take care to avoid the following:—

(a) Including undertakings as orders—if a provision cannot be included in the body of the order it should be expressed as an undertaking or be contained in a separate agreement between the parties. The use of side letters should generally be discouraged.

(b) Asking the court to make an order for which it does not have jurisdiction.

(c) Overlooking the absence of a decree of any sort.

(d) Omitting time limits or penalties, or references to interest.

(e) Creating a strict settlement unknowingly.

8.4 The solicitor should always have in mind later problems which may arise with conveyancing or possible future mortgage applications of either party. Responsibility for the mortgage, community charge or insurance and any arrears together with necessary repairs to the property should be provided for. For further guidance *see* Hayes and Battersby *Property Adjustments: Further Thoughts on Charge Orders* (1986) Fam Law 142.

8.5 The solicitor should consider the most appropriate manner of one spouse retaining an interest in the property. The alternatives are:

    (a)   A *Mesher* order

    (b)   A charge for a fixed sum or preferably a charge for a proportion of the proceeds of sale, or if the property is not being sold of the value of the property.

8.6   If this type of order is made provision should be made for who is to value the property, giving credit to the occupant for any improvements or repairs and the rights of the parties in relation to redemption of the charge. The taxation implications of each type of order should also be discussed with the client.

8.7   The solicitor should also consider with the client the implications of section 8 of the Social Security Act 1990 and the forthcoming provisions of the Child Support Bill before agreeing a consent order.

8.8   Before lodging a consent order with the court a copy of it should be sent to the client and it is advisable to include in the letter an explanation of the terms of the order in simple language. If the client is settling contrary to the solicitor's advice this advice should be clearly stated in the letter.

8.9   Lodging draft consent orders at the court without the necessity of attendance is a useful method of saving costs. This of course depends on care being taken to ensure that the order does not contain errors as this will only lead to an increase in costs due to the need to either return the document to the solicitor or arrange for a short hearing before the District Judge.

8.10 When lodging a consent order at court, if it is agreed that claims by the respondent should be dismissed, Form D13 should also be lodged at court marking it 'for dismissal purposes only'.

8.11 A set of precedents for consent orders for financial relief has been prepared by the Solicitors Family Law Association and can be obtained from Mary I'Anson, PO Box 302, SFLA Keston, Kent BR2 6EZ, DX 86853 Locksbottom (tel. 0689 850227) at a cost of £15 for members of the association and £25 for non-members.

Evans v Evans (Practice Note)
Family Division (26 January 1990)

Booth J. This is a wife's application for ancillary relief following upon a divorce. She seeks for herself a clean financial break from the husband and for the two minor children of the family who live with her she seeks periodical payments. The case has caused me anxiety because of the enormity of the costs which have been incurred in comparison with the assets which are available to meet the needs of the parties. On the husband's side the costs amount in all to £35,000 and on the wife's side they are estimated at £25,000. The available assets consist broadly of two properties both subject to mortgages which are the homes of the respective parties and the husband's shareholding in a small company which provides his livelihood and that of the children and which will not be sold in the foreseeable future. The wife is legally aided and has no independent means. It will thus be seen that the costs are out of all proportion to the assets.

This is by no means an isolated case in this respect. The situation recurs again and again when the court finds itself unable to make appropriate provision for the parties and their children because of their liability for legal costs and it is a matter of the gravest concern to all judges. With the concurrence of the President of the Family Division I shall commence my judgment with some general guidelines to be followed by the practitioner in the preparation of a substantial ancillary relief case.

1 Affidavit evidence should be confined to relevant facts and should not be prolix or diffuse. Each party should normally file one substantive affidavit dealing with the matters to which the court should have regard under section 25 of the Matrimonial Causes Act 1973, as substituted by section 3 of the Matrimonial and Family Proceedings Act 1984, and matters which are material to the application. If any further affidavit is necessary it should be confined to such matters as answering any serious allegation made by the other party, dealing with any serious issue raised or setting out any material change of circumstances.

2 Inquiries made under rule 77 (now FPR, r 2.63) of the Matrimonial Causes Rules 1977 should, as far as possible, be contained in one comprehensive questionnaire and should not be made piecemeal at different times.

3 Wherever possible valuations of properties should be obtained from a valuer jointly instructed by both parties. Where each party instructs a valuer then reports should be exchanged and the valuers should meet in an attempt to resolve any differences between them or otherwise to narrow the issues.

4 While it may be necessary to obtain a broad assessment of the value of a shareholding in a private company it is inappropriate to undertake an expensive and meaningless exercise to achieve a precise valuation of a private company which will not be sold: see *P v P* [1989] 2 FLR 241.

5 All professional witnesses should be careful to avoid a partisan approach and should maintain proper professional standards.

6 Care should be taken in deciding what evidence, other than professional evidence, should be adduced and emotive issues which are not material to the case should be avoided. Where affidavit evidence is filed the deponents must be available for cross-examination on notice from the other side.

7 Solicitors on both sides should together prepare bundles of documents for use at the hearing and should reach agreement as to what should be included and what excluded: duplication of documents should always be avoided.

8   A chronology of material facts should be agreed and made available to the court.

9   In a substantial case it may be desirable to have a pre-trial review to explore the possibility of settlement and to define the issues and to ensure readiness for hearing if a settlement cannot be reached.

10 Solicitors and counsel should keep their clients informed of the costs at all stages of the proceedings and, where appropriate, should ensure that they understand the implications of the legal aid charge: the court will require an estimate of the approximate amount of the costs on each side before it can make a lump sum award: see *Practice Direction (Divorce Registry: Lump Sum Award)* [1982] 1 WLR 1082.

11 The desirability of reaching a settlement should be borne in mind throughout the proceedings. While it is necessary for the legal advisers to have sufficient knowledge of the financial situation of both parties before advising their client on a proposed settlement, the necessity to make further inquiries must always be balanced by a consideration of what they are realistically likely to achieve and the increased costs which are likely to be incurred by making them.

Appendix 8   Example of domestic violence checklist

I   *First Interview*

1 **Client Details**
Name:
Address:
Children:
Home (tenancy or owned)—in whose name
Married/Unmarried
Has partner left and if so when?

2 **Incidents**
Dates:
Details:

3 **Description of assailant**
Physical:
Habits:
Photos if possible.

4 **Injuries**
Have you seen them?
Photograph if possible.

5 **Medical Information**
Hospital:
When:
Where:
Doctors:
When:
Where:
If neither, sent doctor if there are injuries.

6 **Details of why application needs to be *ex parte***

7 **Signed forms of authority re medical or legal papers.**

8 **Sign Legal Aid forms. Apply Legal Aid by telephone if appropriate.**

9 **Arrange representation at Court as appropriate.**

II   *Paperwork*

N16A (Notice of Application)
N16   (Draft Order)
Notice of Issue of Legal Aid
Affidavit (ready to swear or sworn)

Medical report if available (in case of assault/trespass, Particulars of Claim and Default Summons)

All cases top plus two copies.

III   *At Court*

1   ***Ex parte***
Contact court to warn coming and ensure Judge is available.
Arrange meet client 30 minutes early.
Go through Affidavit (amend if necessary).
Court Office to swear (no fee).
Issue papers.
Collect Order (or make arrangements for Enquiry Agent to do so).
Check Order is correct.
Serve personally (within two clear days of return date (if applicable)).
NB If Power of Arrest serve Police Station after personal service on Respondent.

2   **On Notice**
Serve all paperwork on other side at least two clear days before Hearing.

Appendix 9 Precedent letter explaining legal aid

Dear

Re: *Legal aid*

As you know, you have recently put in an application for legal aid to assist you with the fees of your case. Legal aid is administered by the Legal Aid Board who will decide both whether your case has sufficient merit to warrant legal aid being granted to you and whether you come within the financial limits to be eligible.

If you are working your papers will be sent to the DSS, who will assess whether you are financially eligible for legal aid, and if so, whether you should pay a contribution or not. In order to make an assessment they may be sending you a booklet which you must complete and return to them together with any forms that they ask your employers to fill in and return.

Please note that if you are married and living with your spouse, or living with someone as though you are married, you must include their financial details on the form in the column marked 'partner'. If you are separated, living alone, or your spouse or partner is your opponent in this case, you should complete the form with details of your own finances only.

If it is decided that you should pay a contribution out of your income, you will have to pay over the life of the Legal Aid Certificate. If you have to pay a contribution out of savings, you will have to pay one lump sum immediately.

If you recover or preserve money because of the help which legal aid has afforded you, then you may have to repay some of that money to the Legal Aid Board to cover the amount of your legal aid costs. If you recover £2,500 or less, you will not have to repay anything. Any amount over that is chargeable to the Legal Aid Board towards your legal aid costs.

If an order is made that you stay in the matrimonial home, which you own or expect to own after the court case, the Legal Aid Board will take a charge on that property for the amount of their costs. In a matrimonial case, if you have recovered money which you will use to buy a house, under certain circumstances, the Legal Aid Board will defer the repayment of their costs and put a charge on the new property. Normally you must buy a house within twelve months of the date of the court order. If the Legal Aid Board agree to defer payment of their costs and to place a charge on your property, they will charge you interest at 8 per cent per year (*as at 1 September 1993—check current rate with the Legal Aid Board*). You may make arrangements with them to pay this if you want, otherwise it will be added to the original capital sum.

In completing your legal aid application, you have undertaken that any change in your personal or financial circumstances will be notified to the Legal Aid Board by you forthwith, and that you will co-operate with the Legal Aid Board and the DSS promptly.

If you are granted Legal Aid and it is subsequently revoked, you are liable for the full amount of any costs incurred.

We trust that the contents of this letter are understood. If you have any questions arising from the letter, please contact us.

Yours faithfully,

Index